Champions Are Everywhere -The Schedules

Keith Livingstone

ISBN: 1508841349

ISBN-13:978-1508841340

DEDICATION:

"It is not the critic who counts; not the man who points out how the strong man stumbles, or where the doer of deeds could have done them better. The credit belongs to the man who is actually in the arena, whose face is marred by dust and sweat and blood; who strives valiantly; who errs, who comes short again and again, because there is no effort without error and shortcoming; but who does actually strive to do the deeds; who knows great enthusiasms, the great devotions; who spends himself in a worthy cause; who at the best knows in the end the triumph of high achievement, and who at the worst, if he fails, at least fails while daring greatly, so that his place shall never be with those cold and timid souls who neither know victory nor defeat."

~Theodore Roosevelt

ENTHUSIASM

"Don't ask what the world needs.

Ask what makes you come alive, and go do it.

Because what the world needs is people who

have come alive."

Howard Thurman

DISCIPLINE:

Do you not know that in a race

all the runners run,

but only one gets the prize?

Run in such a way as to get the prize.

St Paul (Saul) of Tarsus;
Apostle, Endurance Animal,
Early Athletics Writer

ACKNOWLEDGMENTS:

My brother Colin, a unique man and coach
(he did the cartoons!); our family and friends;
especially my wife, Saint Joanne Livingstone
of the Divine Order of Wives Everywhere, and of
course the late, great Arthur Lydiard who got the
ball rolling.
I hope we're respectfully polishing your gem
of a system to the level it deserves.

Keith Livingstone

CONTENTS

"Champions Are Everywhere"

New Zealand's late, legendary athletics coach, Arthur Lydiard, was named 'Coach of the Twentieth Century' by Runners World. Arthur died in Houston in 2004, aged 87, while touring North America on a speaking tour.

From humble beginnings fostered initially only by a desire to get himself fit for playing club rugby in the late 1940s, he gradually put together an endurance training system that he tested on himself, which resulted in him becoming a New Zealand marathon champion and Commonwealth/Empire Games representative at an age when most men of the era assumed they were 'past it' for such pursuits. Over time, he acquired several enthusiastic pupils from his local neighbourhood, and by the mid-1950's he had his system "ready to go".

So successful was Arthur with his training of 'ordinary' local kids, that he coined the phrase "Champions are Everywhere- they just have to be trained correctly!" When I grew up in the running culture of the 1970s, it was accepted routinely that large volumes of steady running mileage could turn pack-runners into championship contenders. Two of my peers who were 'good' but not 'outstanding' at national junior level went on to international and Olympic marathon representation with another six years of steady endurance work under their belts, while at the same time recording very respectable track times over 5,000m and 10,000m.

The Lydiard method enabled a runner to be at his or her best on the day that mattered most, often able to run as either a 'stayer' or as a 'sprinter'. The system created tough, calloused athletes who were able to win off any pace.

For instance, the ruthless Murray Halberg won the Empire Games 3-mile title in Perth in 1962 with a 53.8 second last 440 yards (402.3 metres!), which was just over a second slower than his best 440 yards race time! Yet, four years earlier, in the Cardiff Empire Games of 1958, Halberg applied a totally different 'tactic': he stranded the entire field by striking hard three laps out, which he repeated again in winning the Rome Olympic Games 5000m title in 1960. Halberg also ran times of 3:38.8 for 1500m and 3:57.5 for the mile, on cinders, in 1958. Any modern-era middle distance athlete will know just how good those times still are.

Most of Lydiard's original students ('Arthur's Boys') are still healthy and well today, in their late 70's or early 80's, and several of them won Olympic medals and set world records. Perhaps the most famous Lydiard athlete was triple Olympic gold medallist Peter Snell, who is now Sir Peter Snell, PhD, a renowned healthy-aging and cardiology researcher based in Dallas Texas. Peter Snell set a world record for the 800m on grass in February 1962, which still stands 53 years later as the NZ and Australasian 800m record. This superlative effort came a week after breaking the world mile record of the time, but remarkably was within nine weeks of a competitive marathon that marked the end of his endurance training phase for that next season.

New Zealand's "golden hour" of Olympic sport occurred on September 2nd, 1960, when favourite Murray Halberg decimated the 5000m field with a withering breakaway from three laps out, half an hour after Olympic novice Snell, ranked 26th in qualifying, broke the Olympic record while beating the world record-holder Roger Moens right on the line in a new Olympic record.

I was lucky enough to spend a pleasant afternoon with adjunct associate professor Sir Peter Snell, PhD, in May 2010, where he showed me where he works as director of the Human Performance Laboratory. With a perfect win record spanning two Olympic Games and one Commonwealth Games, and his subsequent academic career, Peter Snell is likely THE world expert on the physiological, psychological, and mental requirements of peaking for Olympic middle distance events.

Wouldn't it be the obvious thing to respectfully ask this legendary achiever to inspire our future champions? Well; apparently;..NO. The opposite in fact.

Amazingly, Snell's kind offer to help New Zealand athletics with an over-arching national training structure was rejected a number of years ago by an ambitious high-performance sports director, who informed him of his irrelevance.

The price of disrespectfully ignoring the 'elephant in the room' for New Zealand's coaches and athletes for the last fifteen years has been a plummeting descent to an embarrassing level where times that were routinely run at national level by good juniors in New Zealand in the 1970s became more than good enough to win senior national titles.

The larder has been a bit bare in the medal stakes as well for years in New Zealand, with the exception of Michigan-based Olympic 1500m medallist Nick Willis, and some breakthroughs by the Robertson twins, who since they were seventeen years old, chose to live and train in Kenya, where the Lydiard principles are endemic.

Much has been written about the Lydiard system and its application over the years, including several books by Arthur in concert with veteran journalist Garth Gilmour. His phase-by-phase preparation of athletes for seasonal peaks is now known as 'periodization', and is the basis of all successful endurance training routines in use today, across a number of sports and disciplines.

I wrote Healthy Intelligent Training to give a new generation of athletes and coaches an overview of the art, science, and philosophy of Lydiard's methods, with the hindsight of fifty years of sports physiology. Even now, sixty years after Arthur Lydiard had worked out the basic formula by himself, his system stacks up physiologically at every level, and the approach has been responsible for Olympic victories for New Zealand in rowing, kayaking, triathlon, and cycling as well as athletics.

As a youngster I was privileged to grow up in the same neighbourhood as Arthur Lydiard, and for five years from 1976 onwards, I was coached by 1960 Olympic marathon bronze medallist, and 1961 World Cup 10,000m champion, Barry Magee. I went to school with Barry's daughter, Dianne.
After self-coaching myself on the Lydiard system at 17, I won an Auckland Under-18 3,000m title in bare feet, in an Auckland record, winning by over 11 seconds, as well as an Auckland Secondary Schools cross-country championship by over 25 seconds.

Over the ensuing decade I was successful at the elite level, firstly in New Zealand, and then in Australia, with quite a few decisive wins in the three disciplines of cross-country, track, and road running. I moved to Melbourne in 1982 to study chiropractic, and for the next six years while I completed my degree course, I ran with the powerhouse Glenhuntly Athletics Club, whose members included multiple world-record holder and Olympic 10,000m medallist Ron Clarke, as well as marathon great Robert de Castella.

Although I have lived in country Victoria in Australia since 1989, I have helped several athletes reach elite levels in running by 'distance coaching'.Two in particular have gone on to become extremely successful coaches in their own right, with world-class results that make any of my coaching results so far look pretty tame. Both athletes typify the truth that "Champions Are Everywhere".

One athlete who has excelled as an Olympic-level coach is my long-time friend and training partner, Chris Pilone, who has become a coaching 'legend' in New Zealand with his Lydiard-based Olympic triathlon programme for 2004 Athens Olympics gold medallist Hamish Carter. Nowadays, Chris competes at the elite level in road cycling, as well as coaching a select band of runners and triathletes in New Zealand.

The other is my coaching colleague John Meagher, who at over 50 years of age is still a force to be reckoned with at national level over triathlon, cross-country or marathon. John has a world title to his name in age-group Olympic distance triathlon, as well as winning cross-country, 10km road, and half-marathon titles at the World Masters' Games in 2002, setting records that still stand. John, a woodwork teacher, has coached the cross-country and distance squads at Marcellin College, Melbourne, for 20 years, and for the past 16 years they have been undefeated in state and national competition at the team level. Several Australian schoolboy champions have emerged from the squad, as well as one world schools' cross-country individual champion. Several athletes have progressed to running consistently at national elite level in senior competition, with the only difference from their schoolday training being an ability to cope with far more endurance volume each week.

With John, I have managed to refine parts of our system so that we can reliably bring athletes of varying abilities up to very high levels for competition, within a training template based largely on steady endurance running.

What EVERY Athlete has to Understand....

An ACIDIC body can't function optimally. ACIDOSIS depresses the central nervous system, impairs muscle fibre contraction, and impairs all the energy systems of the body. It can depress the imune system, and cause chronic inflammation and injury.

There are THREE major energy systems in the body, each most associated with its own muscle fibre type. Two are very safe to train year-round. Neither of those systems or muscle fibre types is associated with ACIDOSIS.

One is not safe to train year-round. This system is renowned for ACIDOSIS as a by-product. It can reach its maximum capacity within 5 weeks of specific training, and there are several ways to train this system carefully and specifically.

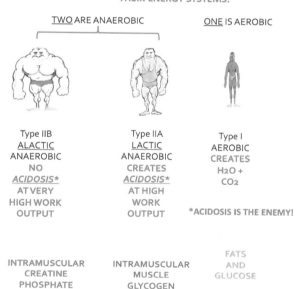

THE THREE MAIN MUSCLE FIBRE TYPES & THEIR ENERGY SYSTEMS:

TWO ARE ANAEROBIC   ONE IS AEROBIC

Type IIB	Type IIA	Type I
ALACTIC	LACTIC	AEROBIC
ANAEROBIC	ANAEROBIC	CREATES
NO	CREATES	H_2O +
ACIDOSIS*	ACIDOSIS*	CO_2
AT VERY	AT HIGH	
HIGH WORK	WORK	
OUTPUT	OUTPUT	*ACIDOSIS IS THE ENEMY!

INTRAMUSCULAR	INTRAMUSCULAR	FATS
CREATINE	MUSCLE	AND
PHOSPHATE	GLYCOGEN	GLUCOSE

More on the Energy Systems....

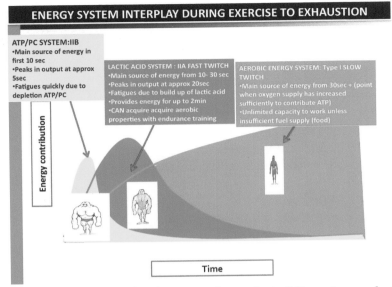

ATP/PC SYSTEM:IIB
•Main source of energy in first 10 sec
•Peaks in output at approx 5sec
•Fatigues quickly due to depletion ATP/PC

LACTIC ACID SYSTEM : IIA FAST TWITCH
•Main source of energy from 10- 30 sec
•Peaks in output at approx 20sec
•Fatigues due to build up of lactic acid
•Provides energy for up to 2min
•CAN acquire acquire aerobic properties with endurance training

AEROBIC ENERGY SYSTEM: Type I SLOW TWITCH
•Main source of energy from 30sec + (point when oxygen supply has increased sufficiently to contribute ATP)
•Unlimited capacity to work unless insufficient fuel supply (food)

Energy contribution

Time

You can see from the diagram above that different muscle fibers and energy systems are recruited in differing time-frames.
The highest-power fibers (IIB) run off a self-topping phosphate high energy system when recovered adequately, and are best exercised with powerful short bursts of activity lasting less than 10 seconds, with plenty of easy recovery. Their metabolism IS anaerobic, but does not produce any acidosis, so it is safe to perform year-round; even while training the type I slow twitch endurance fibers and their fatty acid metabolism.
Training the IIA anaerobic glycolytic fibers intensely with repeated workbouts between 20s and 3 minutes is counter-productive. It competes for training time, and has to be managed very carefully when the correct time comes.

The Energy Systems Training Pyramid

Only one or two key sessions each week would concentrate on the respective energy system or pace being developed. ***Other sessions of the day and week would be restorative and aerobic***, especially the further up the pyramid we get.

> Middle distance high-intensity training is buffered by ample easy aerobic running till the system "neutralizes" again and is ready for more. Easy days are generally run the day before and after a high intensity session. Sometimes two or three easy days might be necessary. Application of the principles will vary according to the individual and the coaching overview.

> Distance Preparation (5k-10k) would have far less emphasis on the top of the pyramid, and the most intense efforts would generally be at VO2 max level..

> Only do one or two of the higher intensity runs a week when in the anaerobic phase; the rest should be steady easy aerobic exercise.

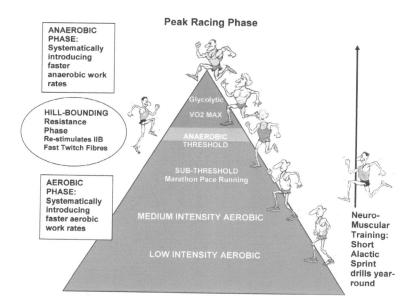

Peak Racing Phase

ANAEROBIC PHASE: Systematically introducing faster anaerobic work rates

HILL-BOUNDING Resistance Phase Re-stimulates IIB Fast Twitch Fibres

AEROBIC PHASE: Systematically introducing faster aerobic work rates

Glycolytic
VO2 MAX
ANAEROBIC THRESHOLD
SUB-THRESHOLD Marathon Pace Running
MEDIUM INTENSITY AEROBIC
LOW INTENSITY AEROBIC

Neuro-Muscular Training: Short Alactic Sprint drills year-round

The HITSYSTEM Training Overview: a templated version of Lydiard.

The Lydiard system relies on methodically building the aerobic capacity and oxygen uptake of the body by steady state endurance speed before leading into a resistance phase of hill exercises for several weeks, followed by time-trials and specific anaerobic glycolytic track training.

Several major things occur after a substantial block of endurance training in the lower intensities:

1. There is an increase in the 'steady state' of the body, whereby more distance can be covered for the same perceived effort.
2. The body utilizes far more fat as fuel than previously , so that it is possible to exercise at 80% of maximal exertion without touching carbohydrate stores. In essence, the slow twitch fibers become prolific, and metabolize fats for energy
3. The capillary system becomes very dense through the muscle fibre beds. This enables much more oxygen, and fuel, to be exchanged at low pressure straight into and out of working muscle cells.

In the first few years of training, it was expected that whatever level of performance had been reached at the end of the previous track racing season could be surpassed easily early in the next track season with another 5 or 6 months' training. After several years the aerobic comfort level exceeds the former racing level.

1. Increasing oxygen uptake

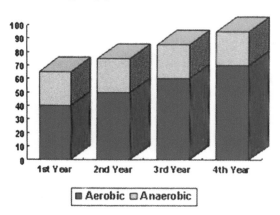

Courtesy Nobby Hashizhume, Lydiard Foundation

2. Much better use of fats as fuel.

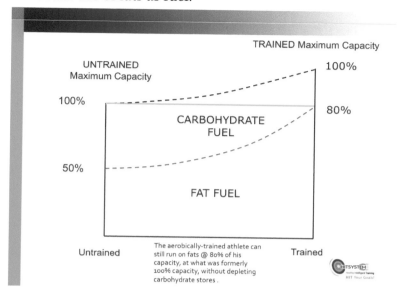

3. Capillarisation of muscle beds in endurance-exercised muscles.

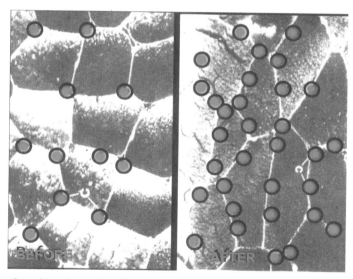

Notice that the cubic _volume_ of capillary exposure based on these pre and post endurance training biopsies has increased 27 times! (Based on the number of capillaries seen in the standard _areas_ viewed, at 11^3 vs 33^3). From 'Distance Running', TAFNEWS, 1979. Dr David Costill

The Basic Approach Described
In Three Paragraphs.

Basically, we are concentrating on each of the three energy systems and their respective muscle fibre types.

1.We train aerobic endurance first, in a long block of training, to ensure that the muscle fibre types used in our specific race distances get adequately 'capillarised'. This will ensure that working muscle fibers get ample oxygen delivery very deep into their structure, and will also ensure that acidic by-products of very intense exercise in a later phase can be carried away rapidly into the general venous system.

2.This steady training period can be 'livened up' with days where training can exercise the completely opposite end of the muscle fibre type spectrum; the fastest-twitch fibers, the IIB. Yes- these fibers ARE ANAEROBIC, but DO NOT PRODUCE LACTIC ACID. We find it easiest to train this fast energy system and muscle fibre by very short, RELAXED sprints over 60 metres or less, with much longer easy recovery running in-between. During the base period this can be mixed into an enjoyable fartlek session over undulating parkland. (This work was done in weekly fartlek workouts on a hilly golf-course by Lydiard's athletes, after a short warm-up). Faster sprinting is a skill that can be learnt by anyone.

3.The final sharpening for competition will involve very hard training that mimics the stresses of flat-out racing. It is done safely when it is buffered with ample volumes of easy recovery exercise, before and after each tough session. Alactic leg-speed drills continue as part of warm-ups, and very easy aerobic work continues before and after each hard race-specific workout. There is no real need to do more than two hard sessions a week for middle-distance (speed-endurance) athletes, because the body needs to recover and progress after each workout, and the body needs to clear acidic metabolites well away from trained muscles, back to the liver, to be re-badged and recirculated, and this is achieved very well by easy aerobic recovery work after a hard session, as well as the following day.

Exercise Physiology 101:
Changes in the Heart Itself with Aerobic Training:

The heart is the source of life, and it is heavily interweaved into the neurology of exercise. It is modulated by responses to the autonomic nervous system (the nervous control of organs and glands) as well as to hormones, stress levels, and general demands of living. There is a new field of study emerging, named cardioneurology, that indicates that the heart has its own inherent neurology that communicates directly with the brain, and in some sense can influence brain function. The concept of a 'heart-brain' that can profoundly influence hormones and emotions, is now being raised by some serious researchers. It may go some way to explain why heart transplant recipients often say they acquire quirky new tastes once the donor heart has settled into its new neuro-cardio-vascular bed, minus the donor's or the recipient's vagus nerve, or any nerve attachments. The donor heart is 'denervated' yet still functions well, despite missing the requisite autonomic nerve supply. All that's left of the recipient's former heart structure is a specifically tailored remnant of his or her pulmonary vein and a portion of the recipient's right atrial musculature.

The neuro-cardiac axis may well be the 'central governor' of exercise physiology postulated by South African author and researcher Dr Tim Noakes, citing the Nobel Prize winner A.V. Hill, who in the 1920's postulated that **"The enormous output of the hearts of able-bodied men, maintained for considerable periods during vigorous exercise, requires a large contemporary supply of oxygen to meet the demands for energy... When the oxygen supply becomes inadequate, it is probable that the heart rapidly begins to diminish its output, so avoiding exhaustion....We suggest that... either in the heart muscle itself or in the nervous system, there is some mechanism (a governor) which causes a slowing of the circulation as soon as a serious degree of unsaturation occurs."**

Research indicates that 'chronic exercise' (aka endurance exercise) invokes structural changes in the human heart that complement the need for delivering more oxygenated blood, per beat, to the muscles. The left ventricle capacity increases, with a mild hypertrophy or growth in the muscular thickness of the pumping chamber.

Endurance training increases left ventricular volume and ejection, with a moderate thickening of the ventricle wall. Resistance (strength) training increases ventricular muscle thickness and power of ejection, but volume remains unchanged

Response to Volume Overload Training

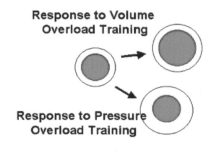

Response to Pressure Overload Training

Measuring Intensity of Exercise Accurately.

Since the great majority of Lydiard-style training is done aerobically, by definition it is also easy on the body and DONE WITH COMFORT. As soon as the athlete starts to huff and puff, he or she has entered another zone and is using different muscle fibre types. So aerobic intensities are pretty easy to plan; exercise is aerobic as long as you're not breathing hard. All the great champions of the past did their spectacular racing off quite repetitive, repeated aerobic bases, and since heart rate monitors only came into regular use in the last 20 years or so, a case can be made to just run without one for the majority of training. HOWEVER some ambitious athletes tend to "race their training", so Heart Rate Monitors will be advised for that sort of athlete , in order to CONTROL efforts.

To accurately plan heart rate zones in training, there are several ways of measuring intensity; only one is truly useful in my opinion, and that is the Karvonen method. This elegant method bases intensity of exercise on a percentage of the difference between a heart rate at rest, and a heart rate at maximal.

Maximal heart rate can be determined by getting the already fit and healthy athlete to run as hard as possible up a hill for at least 3 minutes, and taking a reading near the end. Resting heart rate is best averaged from taking readings on three consecutive mornings, while sitting comfortably.

When the body is at rest, the heart is obviously still beating, so the intensity 'at rest' must be quantified usefully as 'zero'. The difference between Resting H.R. and maximal H.R. is known as the Heart Rate Reserve. As one gets fitter, the resting heart rate gets lower and lower, while the maximal heart rate may also get slightly lower as the left ventricle increases in volume in response to endurance training. Here's Arthur showing you this concept, on the next page.

Lydiard training is usually fun and quite 'social'!
"Train. don't Strain" was Arthur's motto.

Heart Rate Zones Defined Simply.

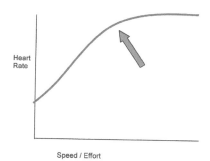

1   As running speed increases, heart rate rises proportionally to a certain point

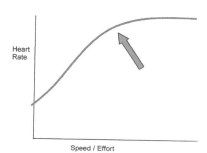

2   This is called the Deflection Point

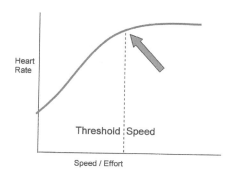

3   The speed run at the deflection point is called Threshold Speed

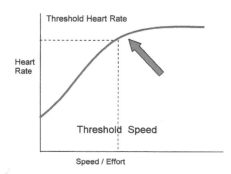

4 The heart rate at the deflection point is called the Threshold Heart Rate

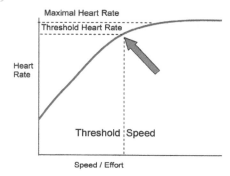

5 The heart rate levels off after this till it reaches maximum

6 Any work after the deflection point is called **maximal work.**

This is also called **ANAEROBIC Work**, meaning performed without oxygen.

Any work before the deflection point is called sub-maximal work.

This is also called AEROBIC work, or ENDURANCE work.

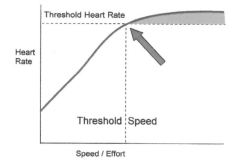

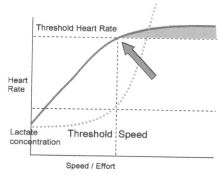

7   At the same time as heart rate rises, LACTATE rises slowly, UNTIL threshold speed is reached. Then it increases exponentially. Threshold occurs at a lactate concentrate of approximately 4 mmol/ litre, though individuals may vary greatly from this average figure.

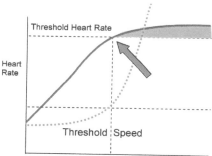

8   If work continues at a high rate, ACIDOSIS will slow the athlete down until exercise is stopped.

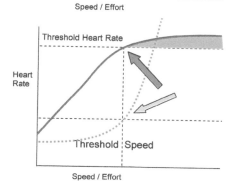

9   This curve is known as the LACTATE CURVE

Note that the deflection point of the heart rate is at Threshold Speed. This point is also the Deflection point for the lactate curve.

Speed / Effort

Note that these diagrams don't illustrate the lowered resting pulse rate following extensive aerobic training.

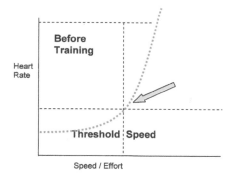

10 Good training will move the deflection point and lactate curve to the right: the athlete will run faster at aerobic speeds

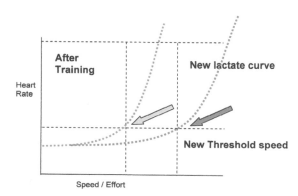

Measuring the Intensity of Exercise with your Heart Rate Monitor.

ALL intensities have their place in the scheme of things in the Lydiard system, especially the lowest intensities, which are considered 'junk mileage' by coaches who do not understand the big picture. The lowest heart rates are extremely beneficial in getting the whole system back into the midly alkali state which good health comes from. (OK: individual organs like the stomach need to have acidic environments, but the bloodstream is most healthy at a mildly alkali level of pH 7.4).

Very low intensity exercise is terrific to deeply perfuse the exercised muscles with oxygenated blood and repair enzymes, and Lydiard used very slow jogging for long periods of up to 3 hours as a means of clearing injuries. I did this myself when I was about 20 years old to clear a nasty hamstring injury caused by a brutal masseur. Two long runs around the 22-mile Waiatarua hill circuit at one hour slower than normal got me nicely back into shape, and I had a creditable performance the next week in a top road race.

It definitely won't make any short-term measureable change in quantifiable things like oxygen uptake or performance, but the immeasureable things like enjoyment of training, general health, strong immunity, and a very deeply developed 'low-pressure delivery and extraction system via fine capillary networks' are worth thinking about.

Lydiard developed a very useful system to describe the required intensity of training efforts, and they ranged from simply 'jogging' to

1) ¼ effort (bread and butter zone where most aerobic training would take place, including long runs), to
2) ½ effort (more of an upper aerobic tempo) to
3) ¾ effort (useful for pushing up the maximal aerobic capacity, just below the anaerobic threshold which is virtually racing tempo) , to
4) 7/8 effort (race-practice time-trial without going all-out) to
5) Full effort (only in races).

The heart rate monitor can be used to describe these intensities very accurately, however I believe it is much better, if one can, to intuitively run at set parameters by 'feel' once you've used the heart rate monitors. When I was training years ago, I could always tell someone how far I had run if I knew how long I had taken. When I measured courses by car later on, I was usually spot-on. Cruising aerobic speed (1/4 effort) for me was about 6 minutes a mile or 3:43 per kilometre.

The Karvonen Method is the best method to determine intensities of training, and we'll explore the method in the next two pages.

Karvonen Method of estimating heart rate intensity.

As described on page 11, the Karvonen method takes into account the resting heart rate as well as the maximal heart rate.

The example given here is for an athlete who has a resting HR of 45, and a maximal HR of 195, so the heart rate reserve or working capacity of the heart is 150 beats a minute.

60%=(45 + 0.6*150)=135	Most Effective Aerobic zones start here: recovery running
65%=(45 +0.65*150)=142.5	Steady Aerobic Zone
70%=(45 +0.70*150)=150	Sub-Threshold Zone Here
75%=(45 +0.75*150)=157.5	Anaerobic Threshold Intensities start above here
80%=(45 +0.80*150)=165	Working quite hard here
85%=(45 +0.85*150)=172.5	Upper end of anaerobic Threshold
90%=(45 +0.9*150)=180	Too hard for AT, too easy for VO2 max, but tiring nevertheless

Varying the Aerobic Strata

All strata are useful: some for easy recovery from harder work, others for pushing the aerobic ceiling up from below. Lydiard athletes <u>never</u> trained at or above anaerobic threshold on a continuous or deliberate basis while building their aerobic strata.

You'll see that in this graph, based on the Karvonen calculations in the previous table, that the recommended 'strong effort' upper aerobic zone which can safely push the anaerobic threshold up, from below, is called the 'sub-threshold' zone. This is the zone where the body, after time, tends to still be burning mostly fats for fuel, and this is the zone which athletes train in once or twice a week during their build-up phase.

Coincidentally, the perceived exertion of '3/4 effort' is very close to 75-80% exertion on the Karvonen scale. Lydiard pupil and coach Barry Magee says that 'half effort', which is also a useful training zone, would be between 70 and 75% intensity on the Karvonen scale. These efforts are only introduced once the athlete is running the volume easily at '1/4' effort, which corresponds to the 65-70% range.

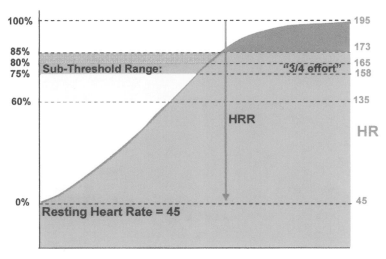

PHASE I: Putting the Lydiard Base together

Lydiard found that a solid block of training devoted almost solely to lower-intensity endurance training got the best results in terms of aerobic development. The aim was to perform as much steady volume in the form of *continuous* aerobic training as possible. These efforts were often run on roads to ensure constant effort and heart rate, and to avoid constraints of wet weather.

Each week there would be be three continuous long runs at steady efforts, and ideally these would include two efforts around 90 minutes (just under, and just over), as well as a much longer effort of over 150 minutes. As long as this longer work was done systematically, and the rules of good nutrition, sleep, and good self-management were applied, an athlete could be GUARANTEED to make a substantial gain in his or her aerobic physiology.

In this graphic TWO sub-threshold runs are done, on a Monday and a Friday, and a fartlek to stimulate leg-speed and give variety to the programme on Wednesday. The athlete has to find the combination that works best for him or her.

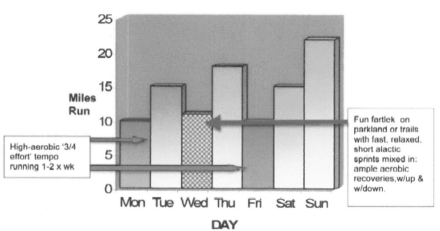

A TYPICAL WEEK OF ENDURANCE TRAINING

High-aerobic '3/4 effort' tempo running 1-2 x wk

Fun fartlek on parkland or trails with fast, relaxed, short alactic sprints mixed in: ample aerobic recoveries, w/up & w/down.

Great care was taken to ensure that NO SUSTAINED INDIVIDUAL EFFORT was even slightly above achieved aerobic comfort zones; if you needed a rest day, your continuous long runs were too fast. However, as one progressed further into one's buildup, the improvement in the steady state of aerobic development meant one would be running much faster for the same relaxed effort. (ie: an athlete's comfortable steady state or '1/4 effort' might be 4:00 a kilometre at the start of a base period, for an elite athlete, and then after a number of weeks it could be 3:40 a kilometre, at the same perceived effort and heart rate). So PERCEIVED EFFORT and training heart rate would remain unchanged as overall speed increased.

This is how a week of endurance training could be planned for an elite athlete; the specific order of sessions doesn't matter too much and the athlete should ensure that he or she finds a routine and favourite circuits that will make the training achievable.
You will notice that it is fine to do relaxed light fast sprints each week while building up aerobic capacity with the steady-state longer runs three times a week. This is fine as it stresses the fastest muscle fibres (IIB) with efforts of less than 10 seconds, with good recoveries, and not the anaerobic lactate system that can be dangerous with respect to acidosis.

The high-aerobic effort session on Saturday in this example is a standard session of pushing up the aerobic capacity at an effort below the anaerobic threshold, and is safe and very effective to use once a week in the aerobic buildup period. You can run one or even two of these efforts safely in a week.

A serious but non-elite athlete may choose to just do the main sessions, and he or she will progress very well with this. If the athlete is serious about his or her goals, he or she will fit this around a full-time job if necessary. There have been plenty of world-class athletes who had full-time employment, and it gives a structure to the training day and week.

Day of week	AM Session	Main Session	Duration	Purpose
Monday	30 mins easy jog	Easy running	About 60 mins	Active recovery
Tuesday	30 mins easy jog	Varied hilly circuit	About 80 mins steady	Endurance run
Wednesday	30 mins easy jog	Fun Fartlek on rolling parkland	About 60 mins with 20 w/up, 20 cool-down	Light alactic sprints and faster work
Thursday	30 mins easy jog	Varied hilly circuit	About 95 mins steady	Endurance run
Friday	30 mins easy jog	Easy running	About 60 mins	Active recovery
Saturday	30 mins easy jog	'3/4 Effort' run	Work up to 60 minutes of this at a constant high-aerobic effort	Push up Aerobic Capacity safely
Sunday		LONG RUN	About 2hrs2hr30	Burning fats: Capillarisation

This sort of training can be done around a full-time job by anyone who wants to seriously improve. It can be kept going for months on end if necessary. I used to average about 120-130 miles per week by running to work for my morning runs, and then doing my longer runs at night on the way home. It requires a bit of juggling with transporting clothes, as well as a shower facility at your place of work, but that's one way of automatically accruing the necessary volume of work. At one place of work I used to run every lunchtime with a lunchtime joggers group, and then walk the short distance home in the city centre, and go on my longer training runs from there. You'll find a way.

Your 26 week/ 6 month Training Plan Overview

6-month training overview for track peak at National Championships.

Increasing intensity of main sessions

Week 26.

Week 25. Ending 28/9/14. **General aerobic recovery from completed winter season**

Week 24.

Week 23.

Week 22.

Week 21. Ending 26/10/ **Start Phase 1; Endurance base**

Week 20. BUILDING VERY DEEP CAPILLARY BEDS, INCREASING CAPACITY TO

Week 19. FLUSH METABOLITES OF EXERCISE, INCREASING DENSITY OF

Week 18. MITOCHONDRIA, RAISING THE ABILITY TO UNDERTAKE ENDURANCE

Week 17. EXERCISE TO 80% OF MAXIMAL INTENSITY ON FAT FUELS ALONE.

Week 16. NO SUSTAINED TRAINING ABOVE ANAEROBIC THRESHOLD.

Week 15.

Week 14.

Week 13. Ending 21/12/ **Start Phase 2; Hill Resistance Exercise Phase**

Week 12. SWITCHING FAST TWITCH IIB FIBRES BACK ON

Week 11.

Week 10. Ending 11/1/1 **Start Phase 3; Initial VO2 anaerobic phase**

Week 9. INTRODUCING TOLERANCE OF HIGH LEVELS OF SYSTEMIC ACIDOSIS

Week 8. **Weekly Races**

Week 7. "   "

Week 6. Ending 1/2/15 **Start Phase 4; Final Phase**

Week 5. TOLERANCE FOR VERY HIGH LEVELS OF LOCAL ACIDOSIS

Week 4. Ending 1/3/15. **State Championships**

Week 3. Maintain and sharpen more in these these weeks

Week 2.

Week 1. Ending 29/3/1 **National Championships**

Plan back from here

NOTE: Steady recovery-based aerobic work continues all-season long, in each phase, on Mondays, Wednesdays, Fridays, and Sundays. This gives CONSTANCY to the template as we progress through the season. **The increasing intensities in each phase pertain ONLY to specific sessions, usually done on Tuesdays or Saturdays.**

"So simple that no one can understand it" (Rich Englehart)

This diagram clearly shows the concept that is fundamental to the HITSYSTEM interpretation of Lydiard's wonderful wholistic overview. It's "so simple that no one can understand it", according to Rich Englehart, a long-time acolyte of Arthur Lydiard and his philosophy.

In this diagram, I have attempted to show how simply I regard the whole philosophy, tied into the physiology. After thirty-plus years of studying the physiology of exercise, specifically for running, but applicable in theory to any sport, I now have put into a simple diagram, which I'll explain afterwards so you'll see how simple it all really is.

THE TWO GREAT SECRETS OF LYDIARD TRAINING
1   The greater the Intensity of the main sessions in your phase of training, the more low-intensity recovery work is required.
2   Significant aerobic volume can still be done right until the peak

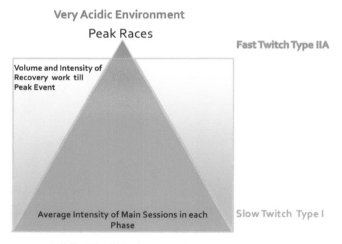

Very Acidic Environment
Peak Races
Fast Twitch Type IIA

Volume and Intensity of Recovery work till Peak Event

Average Intensity of Main Sessions in each Phase
Slow Twitch Type I

Mildly Alkali Environment

OK: the astute reader will note that milk itself is ever so slightly acidic, with a pH of 6.9, but compared to vinegar it is much more alkali. You get the point. The body's energy, enzyme, and hormonal systems operate best in an oxygen-rich, mildly alkali environment of pH 7.365-7.40.

You'll notice that the type IIB explosive muscle fibers, are not included in the diagram. That's because healthy training towards a planned peak phase is a war between type I fibers and Type IIA fibers, aerobic metabolism and systemic acidosis. Total volume of training stays much the same as we move towards a Lydiard-based peak, however the intensity of most of it (recovery running) gets easier and easier as we move through the season towards the planned peak. The high-intensity IIA training volume gets smaller and smaller, but more and more intense, as we near a peak.

The type IIB fibers are still trained each week though, but if they're trained specifically and for no longer than 10 seconds each time, they won't affect the net balance of acid/alkali in training in any harmful way. Notice in the diagram that as we move through the phases towards the peak, more and more easy, restorative, aerobic type I muscle fiber activity is necessary to sandwich any very high intensity work.

For an absolute peak for middle-distance anaerobic glycolytic/lactic tolerance events like 800m, the extremely easy restorative work can drop away, steadily, without stopping abruptly, with the long easy runs dropping by 20% two weeks out, then another 20% one week out. So a 2-hour (120 minute) easy run on parkland or trails can become 1 hour 36 minutes, then 77 minutes one week out (OK-75 will do…but you get the idea…). The aerobic 'work' becomes almost pitifully slow and easy, in order to counter and recover properly from the high intensity work.

PHASE II: THE HILL RESISTANCE PHASE

Lydiard really saw this as a transition time where the very fine development of the aerobic system was maintained while the leg muscles were strengthened by resistance exercise. He even said that this work could satisfactorily be done in a gym if hills weren't available (and while coaching in Denmark, which has a very flat topography, he was forced to adapt gym-based work to develop the leg strength he was after.).

Lydiard certainly wasn't opposed to the notion of specific strength training for athletes, but as he had to deal with athletes who often had other important demands on their time, training had to be time-efficient. He was also concerned about possible imbalances in lifting techniques causing gym-based injuries and felt that hill-running and bounding drills, done correctly, exercised the prime movers required for fast and very fast running in a far more specific manner that delivered exquisite results.

Not only middle distance runners benefited from this phase. US track coach Jim Bush, coach of 1992 Olympic 400m champion Quincy Watts, and 110m high hurdles champion Mark Currier, said *"I owe my success as a long sprint coach to Lydiard's hill training."*

But where to start? A *gradual transition* into this new form of work with 'no nasty surprises' is always the Lydiard way of doing things. It just so happens that one of the best ways to prepare the athlete going into the final sharpening phase is by gradually working in 'hill exercises' several days a week, while maintaining aerobic development with one or two longer runs each week as well. These are basically form drills that are performed uphill. Lydiard ended up with three types of hill exercise, each with a different purpose.

1.**Steep Hill Running**- slow forward progress with accentuated full leg and foot extension with each stride.
Probably best done within an alactic (10 seconds or less) time-frame ie: 50m or less, uphill

---

2. Hill Bounding- long bounding strides like a triple jumper, concentrating on full rear leg extension

3. Hill springing- very slow forward progress, with most movement coming from the ankle flexors. Because of this very slow exercise, it can be done over a longer time without undue problems.

How to do it:

Start the very first hill exercise session with a good warmup, and some relaxed leg-speed strides beforehand, with full recoveries. Then try two of each of the exercises as described here, concentrating on good form uphill. You can build the number of exercises up over several weeks, and group the exercises into sets, so that by the end of the hill exercise phase, you are performing quite a few repetitions on your hill exercise days, as well as maintaining quite a reasonable aerobic volume on other days. (Images courtesy Lydiard Foundation).

1.Steep hills running

2. Hill-bounding

3. Hill-springing.

In addition to these exercises, the downhill slopes can be utilized for fast striding with high turnover, after some recovery at the top of the slope.

(For more on these, you'll have to read Pages 108 onwards in the book, 'Healthy Intelligent Training')

Hill exercises can stimulate the nervous system far more than anticipated, as even mild bounding uphill has a very excitatory effect on the neuromuscular system. These days, this principle is known as 'plyometric exercise', and everyone from the pony-tailed 'Personal Trainer' to the Russian sports scientist knows about it, however it was first worked into an organized, periodized approach well over 55 years ago!

This is is what hills can do!

Both Keino and Vasala were big proponents of hill exercises. Vasala did them right into his final preparations for the 1972 Munich Olympics1500m, where off a last 800m of 1:48.9, he ran a devastating last 120m to head off Kipchoge Keino.

How a Lydiard-Based Hill Exercise Phase could look for an elite athlete in the middle of a hill phase:

The morning very easy aerobic runs aid in recovery, and it is a good idea if you can fit them into your schedule if you want to do the best you can. Even the slowest running paces will still utilize the aerobic systems, and help to return your blood acid/alkali balance to a more healthy neutral level. Easy morning runs will help maintain the very high levels of aerobic enzymes and the mitochondria that support them. All are beneficial to the general health of the athlete.

Naturally, the PRINCIPLES of adaptation and gradual introduction of new types of exercise in each phase should be observed sensibly.

Day of week	AM Session	Main Session	Duration	Purpose
Monday	30 mins easy jog	Easy running	About 60 mins	Active recovery
Tuesday	30 mins easy jog	Hill circuits x2	About 80 mins	Fast twitch IIB muscle fibre reactivation.
Wednesday	30 mins easy jog	Easy running	About 60 mins	Active recovery
Thursday	30 mins easy jog	Hill circuits x2	About 80 mins	IIB muscle fibre Reactivation.
Friday	30 mins easy jog	Easy running	About 60 mins	Active recovery
Saturday	30 mins easy jog	'3/4 Effort' run, gradually giving way to a shorter A.T. effort by wk.4	Work up to 60 minutes of this at a constant high-aerobic effort	Push up Aerobic Capacity safely
Sunday		LONG VERY EASY RUN	About 2hrs-2hr30	Endurance run; Long and relaxed, maintaining good form and rhythm.

An Overview of How to Safely Phase In the Hill Exercises over a few weeks.

How To Implement Hill Exercises enroute to specific anaerobic track preparation (Just an example...)

As with each of the phases, introduce the new work gradually, and ALWAYS concentrate on good technique. Here's one way of gradually introducing hill exercises over several weeks, without blowing your barn doors off!

Obviously, these specific hill exercises will only be done on two or three days a week (although if done correctly they can be safe enough to do daily, if other easy longer running sandwiches the hill sessions).

Week One Workouts: After 30 minutes of easy aerobic running, and several alactic strideouts over 60m or less, do two of each of the individual exercises, with an easy minute of recovery jogging after each, and two minutes of jogging between each set of two repetitions. Jog easily after completion for a further 30 minutes. (There will be a total of 6 hill exercises , done twice in the first week)

Week Two Workouts: After 30 minutes of easy aerobic running, and several alactic strideouts over 60m or less, do three of each of the individual exercises, with an easy minute of recovery jogging after each, and two minutes of jogging between each set of three repetitions. Jog easily after completion for a further 30 minutes. (There will be a total of 9 hill exercises , done twice in the second week)

Week Three Workouts: After 30 minutes of easy aerobic running, and several alactic strideouts over 60m or less, do four of each of the individual exercises, with an easy minute of recovery jogging after each, and two minutes of jogging between each set of four repetitions. Jog easily after completion for a further 30 minutes. (There will be a total of 12 hill exercises, done twice in the third week)

Week Four Workouts: After 30 minutes of easy aerobic running, and several alactic strideouts over 60m or less, do five of each of the individual exercises, with an easy minute of recovery jogging after each, and two minutes of jogging between each set of five repetitions. Jog easily after completion for a further 30 minutes. (There will be a total of 15 hill exercises, done twice in the fourth week)

Start to introduce anaerobic threshold work just a little bit. Change Saturday 3/4 effort high-aerobic session to Anaerobic Threshold pace that corresponds with best realistic race pace that can be held for 50-60 minutes. Those sessions should only be for about 20 minutes of tempo, after a warmup of 20 minutes, followed by a cool-down of 20 minutes. This is a step up from the intensity of the high-aerobic intensity sub-threshold runs that have been performed weekly, for weeks on end throughout the aerobic base phase, and these introduce the IIA fibers with their glycolytic anaerobic metabolism into the progression of intensities. Only a couple of weeks with these runs is necessary before introducing the next phase, if the aerobic base has been built correctly.

PACING YOURSELF ACCURATELY!

For most athletes, the answer isn't how FAST, but at what EFFORT should one train?

In a nutshell, the GREAT MAJORITY of training for most athletes will be bread and butter aerobic training, either as part of an endurance base, or as a means of recovering from intense work as one lifts intensities through a season. To get the necessary high volume of aerobic work in, it's best that the aerobic phase is made as interesting as possible, with a number of differing courses, surfaces, and different emphases wthin the aerobic strata; from very low-level and restorative to quite high-level, pushing the anaerobic threshold "up from below."

The spectacular hard, fast repetitions and intervals represent only a couple of the final bricks in the wall, and usually only a hard effort session here, and another one there, with easy days in between, are necessary to get to one's best for the season, because actual racing is the most specific speed-endurance training an athlete can get. 100% race-specific.

The British Miler's Club did a survey of its members in recent years, and found that personal bests over 800m or 1500m were most likely to occur after 5 races at either distance. Those races can be developmental before the peaking period. The value in a number of competitive races before the 'big one' may be found in hardening the athlete to 'another day at the office', and fine-tuning his or her best warm-up and race strategies. Each race has to be viewed as a rehearsal of the planned peak event, and expectations initially should be only of a solid competitive performance. Things do get better quite quickly though.

If the season is well-constructed, the athlete will feel himself improving noticeably week by week, to the point that he can hardly wait to 'strut his stuff' in the big competition. A well-planned Lydiard preparation will take the athlete on a conveyor-belt like ride once the specific work commences.

American distance coach Jack Daniels is famous for his quantifying the question of "how fast should I train?" with his 'Vdot tables'. Daniels , a former modern pentathlon Olympic silver medallist, has spent over fifty years behind the scenes as an exercise physiologist and coach. I hereby defer to Daniels's vast experience in this area, with a table based on his V Dot tables, with his permission.

Many new athletes don't realise that their performance expectations at any distance can be predicted confidently from established recent performances.

Across the board, the ratios of relative performance over varying distances from 800m up are much the same for a world-class athlete or a well-conditioned club runner. They're humans, and both obey the basic laws of physiology, with set limits that dictate optimal training and racing speeds.

I have seen many athletes over the years who mistakenly confuse their ability to tolerate fast, hard work and a mountain of acidosis with an ability to run well in a race. One athlete now suffers severe health issues from this approach, unfortunately, requiring a pacemaker at only 30 years of age.

THE JACK DANIELS TRAINING PACES AND VO2 MAX INTERVAL TRAINING

AEROBIC PROFILE: (based on work by Jack Daniels, PhD, exercise physiologist, US Olympic running coach)

This table indicates current potential at other distances if trained for correctly. Different athletes will have different profiles.

If strong on short distances but weaker on long, threshold must be trained at the slower zone. Threshold is the pace we can race 50-60 minutes at.

VO2 max is the pace we can race 8-12 minutes at. Train @ 5k pace (95% max). Reps: 1500 pace. Practice good form and mechanics. Fast reps: controlled 800 race pace or faster.

Sub-labels: 1500/Mile = **REP PACE**; 3000/5000 = **VO2 INTERVAL PACE** "hard"; 15k = **THRESHOLD PACE** "comfortably hard" / "very fast runners:21k pace".

VDOT Racing Level	400	800	1500	Mile	3000	5000	10000	15k	21.1k	42.2k	Fast Reps (800 pace/faster 200:300:400:600, Full recovery)	Reps (1500 pace 200:400:600, Full rec.)	Intervals (5k pace:2-5 min 800:1000:1200, Equal rec./less)	Threshold (15k pace, 5 min-1 hour, 1/5 rec or less)	Easy (Threshold + 40s, Recovery/Long, Constant)
61.0	60.0	2.12	4.30.5	4.52.2	9.41	16.48	34.52	53.32	77.02	2.41.08	33 49 66 99	37 74 111	2.40 3.20 4.00	3.36	4.17-4.36
62.0	59.0	2.10	4.26.0	4.47.3	9.33	16.34	34.23	52.47	75.57	2.38.54	32 48 65 97	36 73 109	2.38 3.18 3.57	3.34	4.15-4.33
63.0	58.0	2.07.6	4.21.5	4.42.4	9.25	16.20	33.55	52.03	74.54	2.36.44	31 47 64 96	36 72 108	2.36 3.15 3.54	3.32	4.12-4.31
64.0	57.0	2.05.4	4.17.0	4.37.5	9.17	16.07	33.28	51.21	73.53	2.34.38	31 46 62 94	35 71 106	2.34 3.13 3.51	3.29	4.10-4.28
65.0	56.5	2.04.3	4.14.7	4.35.1	9.09	15.54	33.01	50.40	72.53	2.32.35	31 46 62 93	35 70 105	2.32 3.10 3.48	3.26	4.07-4.26
66.0	56.0	2.03.2	4.12.5	4.32.6	9.02	15.42	32.35	50.00	71.56	2.30.36	30 46 61 92	34 69 103	2.30 3.07 3.45	3.24	4.05-4.24
67.0	55.0	2.01.0	4.10.3	4.27.7	8.55	15.29	32.11	49.22	71.00	2.28.40	30 45 60 90	34 68 102	2.28 3.05 3.42	3.21	4.02-4.21
68.0	54.5	1.59.9	4.05.7	4.25.3	8.48	15.18	31.46	48.44	70.05	2.26.47	30 45 60 90	33 67 100	2.26 3.02 3.39	3.20	4.00-4.18
69.0	54.0	1.58.8	4.03.5	4.22.9	8.41	15.06	31.23	48.08	69.12	2.24.57	29 44 59 89	33 66 99	2.24 3.00 3.36	3.17	3.57-4.16
69.5	53.5	1.57.7	4.01.2	4.20.4	8.34	14.55	31.00	47.32	68.21	2.23.10	29 44 58 88	32 65 98	2.22 2.58 3.33	3.14	3.55-4.14
70.0	53.0	1.56.6	3.59.0	4.18.0	8.31	14.49	30.49	47.15	67.56	2.22.18	29 43 58 87	32 65 97	2.22 2.58 3.33	3.13	3.53-4.12
70.5	52.5	1.55.5	3.56.8	4.15.6	8.28	14.44	30.38	46.58	67.31	2.21.26	29 43 57 86	32 64 97	2.20 2.56 3.31	3.12	3.51-4.10
71.0	52.0	1.54.4	3.54.5	4.13.2	8.22	14.33	30.16	46.24	66.42	2.19.44	28 43 57 85	32 64 96	2.20 2.55 3.30	3.10	3.50-4.08
72.0	51.5	1.53.3	3.52.2	4.10.7	8.16	14.23	29.55	45.51	65.54	2.18.05	28 42 56 84	31 63 95	2.18 2.53 3.27	3.08	3.47-4.06
73.0	51.0	1.52.2	3.50.0	4.08.3	8.13	14.18	29.44	45.35	65.31	2.17.17	28 42 56 84	31 62 94	2.17 2.51 3.25	3.07	3.46-4.05
74.0	50.5	1.51.1	3.47.8	4.05.9	8.10	14.13	29.34	45.19	65.08	2.16.29	28 42 55 83	31 62 93	2.16 2.50 3.24	3.06	3.45-4.04
75.0	50.0	1.50.0	3.45.5	4.03.5	8.04	14.03	29.14	44.48	64.23	2.14.55	27 41 55 82	30 61 92	2.14 2.49 3.22	3.04	3.44-4.03
76.0	49.5	1.48.9	3.43.2	4.01.1	7.58	13.54	28.55	44.18	63.39	2.13.23	27 41 54 81	30 61 91	2.14 2.48 3.21	3.02	3.42-4.01
77.0	49.0	1.47.8	3.41.0	3.58.6	7.53	13.44	28.36	43.49	62.56	2.11.54	27 41 54 81	30 60 90	2.12 2.45 3.18	3.00	3.40-3.59
78.0	48.5	1.46.7	3.38.8	3.56.2	7.48	13.35	28.17	43.20	62.15	2.10.27	26 40 53 79	29 59 88	2.10 2.43 3.15	2.58	3.38-3.57
79.0	48.0	1.45.6	3.36.5	3.53.8	7.43	13.26	27.59	42.52	61.34	2.09.02	26 39 52 78	29 58 88	2.08 2.41 3.13	2.56	3.36-3.55
80.0	47.5	1.44.5	3.34.2	3.51.4	7.37	13.18	27.41	42.25	60.54	2.07.38	26 39 52 78	29 58 87	2.08 2.40 3.12	2.54	3.35-3.54
81.0	47.0	1.43.4	3.31.9	3.48.9	7.32	13.09	27.24	41.58	60.15	2.06.17	25 38 51 77	28 57 85	2.06 2.38 3.10	2.53	3.33-3.52
82.0	46.5	1.42.3	3.29.7	3.46.5	7.27	13.01	27.07	41.32	59.38	2.04.57	25.5 38 51 77	28 56 84	2.04 2.37 3.08	2.51	3.31-3.50
83.0	46.0	1.41.2	3.27.6	3.44.1	7.23	12.53	26.51	41.06	59.01	2.03.40	25 37.7 50 76	27 55 82	2.02 2.36 3.06	2.49	3.29-3.48
84.0	45.5	1.40.1	3.25.5	3.42.7	7.18	12.45	26.34	40.42	58.25	2.02.24	25 37.5 50 75	27 55 82	2.02 2.34 3.05	2.48	3.27-3.46
85.0	45.0	1.39.0	3.23.5	3.41.3	7.14	12.37	26.19	40.17	57.50	2.01.10	24.7 37 49 74	27 55 81	2.01 2.31 3.03	2.46	3.25-3.48

To use the VDOT Pace Tables, find the established race time and distance nearest your athlete's current level of performance in the RACING TIMES columns on the left side of the table. The row nearest the established performance is the ascribed VDOT level.

How to Do This:

In the example on the left, the athlete has run 15:00 for 5000m, and wants to know what that translates to with the right training for 1500m, and what specific sessions will deliver the possible result. 15:00 for 5000m falls right between two 'VDOT' Racing Levels; 69.0 and 69.5.

So the assumed correct time to aim for will be between the two 1500m times listed on the two rows. Current race potential with correct training will be for a 1500m time between 4:01.2 and 4:03.5. And current 3000m potential will be between 8:34 and 8:41. It's a good idea to set the training paces for the slightly faster levels, as it is realistic and safe to do so, rather than make the HUGE mistake of running flat out at inappropriately fast speeds that don't represent current realistic potential.

Training paces for hard effort days will be in the right-sided columns in the Daniels Chart. Daniels makes a distinction between two types of high intensity work; VO2 Max work and Glycolytic Anaerobic, or 5000m/3000m pace work(INTERVALS) and 1500m/800m pace work (REPETITIONS), respectively.

PHASE III: EARLY ANAEROBIC WORK.
Large volumes of work at VO2 max pace.

After the long, steady aerobic base phase and several weeks of the hill-resistance phase, we introduce anaerobic intensities that will be able to be done for many minutes, with short recoveries, in order to perform enough work to raise levels of acidosis in the whole body to stimulate systemic buffering of acids by the body's bicarbonate systems.

* A raised amount of acid in the body is described as lowering pH, while a raised amount of alkalinity in the body is referred to as raising pH.

VO2-max-paced intervals ideal

• Good Safe Effective Example: For a 15:00 5000m performer:5 x 1000m @ your best 5000m pace/equal jog recovery (ie: 2.5 laps hard/1.5 slow: one interval every 6:00).

• NB: 3000 pace VERY SPECIFIC but very hard. In the case of the 15:00 performer, the 3000m-pace (100% VO2 max) 1000m intervals are to be run only once very comfortable with the 5000m work.

• Intervals b/w 2-3 mins/equal recovery best stimulus: can be done on cc loop or wherever most enjoyable.

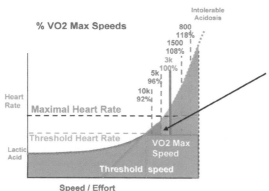

VO2 Max Exercise occurs here, between 3k and 5k pace, before the point where lactate increases exponentially. You can see that VO2 max work is maximal, anaerobic work, well above the anaerobic threshold.

This is most safely trained at 5000m speed or best 15 minute pace (96% VO2 max). Later as one gets fitter it can be trained at 3000m (100% VO2 max) or best 8 minute pace.

PHASE III Early Anaerobic Work
(A): 5000m pace 95%VO2Max INTERVALS:
(First Anaerobic Phase- early track season, after Hills)

This work is performed at actual race-pace speeds for current 5000m potential. These have EQUAL OR SHORTER TIME RECOVERY, which may be done while jogging slowly.

Daniels prefers the early weeks of intervals to be at 5000m pace (95% of VO2 max pace), because there will still be a strong stimulus to VO2 max, and more time in this region can be spent, safely. An ideal workout for a 5000m runner who has run 15:00 may be 5 x 1000m (2.5 laps) @ 3:00 with 1.5 laps jog recovery in 3:00, or a neat 6:00 per interval cycle.

(B): Fast VO2 Max Intervals: 3000m pace '100%VO2 Max' (Don't do too many at this intensity)

The more intense 100% VO2 max session reps for this athlete would be something like 3 x 1000m @ 2:51, and 3:09 recovery would be fine as it makes for a nice round 6:00 unit which is easy to time. As long as the training is reasonably accurate the wisdom of the body will know what to do with it. We need to get the PACE exactly right, and make sure that recoveries are short enough to make a meaty session out of the workout.

PHASE III: EARLY ANAEROBIC WORK.
Large volumes of work at VO2 max pace.

After the long, steady aerobic base phase and several weeks of the hill-resistance phase, we introduce anaerobic intensities that will be able to be done for many minutes, with short recoveries, in order to perform enough work to raise levels of acidosis in the whole body to stimulate systemic buffering of acids by the body's bicarbonate systems.

* A raised amount of acid in the body is described as lowering pH, while a raised amount of alkalinity in the body is referred to as raising pH.

VO2-max-paced intervals ideal

• Good Safe Effective Example: For a 15:00 5000m performer:5 x 1000m @ your best 5000m pace/equal jog recovery (ie: 2.5 laps hard/1.5 slow: one interval every 6:00).

• NB: 3000 pace VERY SPECIFIC but very hard. In the case of the 15:00 performer, the 3000m-pace (100% VO2 max) 1000m intervals are to be run only once very comfortable with the 5000m work.

• Intervals b/w 2-3 mins/equal recovery best stimulus: can be done on cc loop or wherever most enjoyable.

• Advantages of training @ VO2 : A lot of good work can be performed before 'acidosis' causes exercise to stop. A safe and effective way to create large amounts of 'systemic' acidosis, which will stimulate the body's ability to tolerate sustained hard work.

• Disadvantages: Not at rates of power output specific to fast 800m and 1500m running. To achieve this, we have to go harder, and faster, for shorter distances, SPARINGLY, to flood the running muscles with acid, thereby stimulating the bicarbonate buffer system and higher tolerance for severe workloads.

We find that in a track-athletics situation, most athletes re_
to one or two doses of this work, which we set aside for Tues
afternoons, as well as Saturday afternoons,(if not racing in early-
season), for a similar training effect. It is possible to do more of this
work in a week, but across the board, this is not advised because
although the athlete may feel very 'energised' and 'wired' by the high-
stress training demands on the adrenal system, the 'adaptation tank'
will be running low.

We find that most athletes respond well to an "easy-hard-easy-
moderate-easy-hard-long easy" sequence for each of the early
anaerobic weeks. The Thursday sessions in this phase can have a
'suggestion' of what you're trying to train, but nowhere near as much
volume at the level of intensity of Tuesday or Saturday. So after a 20
minute easy warm-up, and then a session of short, fast, relaxed sprints
of 60 metres or less, with easy jog recoveries, we may just do fun
fartlek work or even 'steady laps' for 2000m or 3000m at estimated
anaerobic threshold pace. This will give the acidosis buffers a little
reminder of what is expected, without blowing the barn doors off
with too much of a good thing. The chart following is an example of
a typical Phase III/VO2 max week for a junior athlete attempting a
sub- 4:00 1500m.

This would be for an athlete who had reached a 15:00 5000m, and is
attempting a 1500m in 4:00 or under. This template can be expanded
with morning runs for a senior athlete, as well as longer, very easy
effort continuous runs on Sundays.

ve through the phases, don't be tempted to run harder
...a need to, to achieve a set time. The weather may preclude
...ood training session, or you might be a bit tired on the day
concerned. If you're genuinely low on energy, you may be better
off to just jog for an easy hour, and drop the session. You're
training to race, not racing to race.

Day	Overview	Details	Notes
Mon	Very easy recovery	30-40 mins easy on parkland	
Tue	Tougher effort day tuned @ current 5000m performance level or slightly faster.	5x 1000m @ 2:59, one every 6:00, concentrating on proper form and rhythm, after suitable easy warmup with legspeed drills over 60 metres or less/ full recovery. Last one try for 2:55. If more recovery needed with intervals; may be running above one's current level. Don't run these if can't hold form. Stop session and just jog.	* As the major races approach, the emphasis of these efforts may change to more specific race-pace repetitions at exactly goal pace
Wed	Longer steady run	May range up to 70 min for seniors.	
Thu	Another effort day but not as demanding as Tue. This day is more or less kept as a constant fun speedplay day year-round.	Warmup with plenty of short fast relaxed sprints then enjoyable 'speed-play' fartleks and recoveries on undulating parkland. May be useful to have 2000m of 'steady laps' @ 75s here.(6:15).	* Alactic leg-speed day * Light fartleks and speed play according to feel, or steady lapping to practice concentration.
Frid	Very easy recovery	Usu. Over 30 mins easy on parkland	
Sat	3000m RACE at 8:34 pace,or 5000m in 14:55 or if no race, a strong effort day ie: 16 x 400m @ 68s/ 1 lap recovery jog. Last 400m try to pick pace up in last straight. We are "training to race, not racing to train".**Always leave something in the tank.**	Race: hold 68.5s to 2400m in 6:51, then position oneself over next 400m for good last 200m. Training: Look for consistency of laps at expected goal race pace, with enough recovery to do repetitions with very good technique. Same w/up as Tuesday.	* Often will re-visit cross-country intervals or hill sessions when not racing. All work expected to be carried out with good rhythm and form.
Sun	Always long and very easy over hilly circuits	Juniors usually up to 90 mins if several years on programme. Older athletes often go longer, easily.	* Now the runs become quite a bit easier in intensity to offset the intensity of the harder days.

PHASE IV GLYCOLYTIC ANAEROBIC REPETITIONS:

A: 1500m PACE (Second Anaerobic Phase, before peaking)

Shorter distance efforts at current 1500m potential, with FULL RECOVERY. This recovery must be enough to ensure that technique in the next repetition is excellent.

For a 15:00 5000m runner wanting to obtain a realistic 3:59 1500m, his target times for this form of training could be 200m in 32s/ 400m in 64s, or 600m repetitions in 97s, with FULL RECOVERY. (3:59 for 1500m is a tad faster than 64s per 400m).

Many athletes will find 32s for 200m very easy to do, however ten to twenty repetitions at that pace with perfect form will be a bit more demanding. Another way to make the 32 second 200m reps 'work' the anaerobic systems nicely would be to do things like three sets of (4x200m@32s/28s recovery), with 2 minutes of easy jogging between sets. This is an area where the coach and athlete can be creative at race paces, with differing distances and recoveries at goal race pace. As long as the actual pace is adhered to, and enough recovery is given between work-bouts to ensure good form in the next repetition, you'll be heading in the correct direction.

GLYCOLYTIC ANAEROBIC REPETITIONS:

B: 800m PACE OR SHORTER

Since 800m pace is so much faster than either of the preceding VO2 max interval or 1500m pace repetition paces, it has to be treated with caution. It's quite OK to lie down or jog very slowly to recover from the much higher acid load at the ramped-up speeds. Peter Snell used to lie on his back with his feet up on a steeplechase barrier apparently. These fast repetitions will load up the running muscles with plenty of acidosis, very quickly.

We usually alternate weeks with the 1500m-pace work and the 800m work, as most track seasons will alternate these races each fortnight. Either race distance is useful to toughen the athlete for optimal racing at the other, and logically, if we're racing a 1500m on Saturday, then Tuesday will include 1500m repetitions at 1500m pace, and if it's an 800m race on Saturday, then Tuesday's session is done with FAST REPS at 800m pace or faster.

According to the Daniels Charts, a runner who is capable of 3:59 for 1500m may be capable of 800m in 1:56.6, and straight away we see a sharp increase in pace at the business end of acidosis: the pace drops from 64s per 400m to 58.3s.

This is an almost 10% increase in pace, all the while running into a sea of acidosis if continued, so it's suggested that recoveries with the fast repetitions are very long and easy to ensure that enough of the work at goal pace can be done with good technique to make a significant stimulus.

Peter Snell used to lie down on the grass, with his feet up on a steeple chase barrier, if need be. If recovery is poor with ragged technique due to acidosis, without a proper aerobic base and good recovery, all we're training the mind and body to do is associate those achievable race speeds with neuromuscular breakdown and failure.

The progression in pace from Intervals (5000m pace) to Fast Intervals (3000m pace) to Repetitions (1500m pace) to Fast Repetitions (800m pace) goes as follows, for a 15:00 5000 m performer at a VDot of 69.5:

5000m pace: 72s/lap

3000m pace: 68s/lap (5.8% drop)

1500m pace: 64s/lap (6.2% drop)

800m pace:58s/lap (9.8% drop)

PHASE IV: GLYCOLYTIC ANAEROBIC REPETITIONS: 4:00 1500m PACE.

As one gets into late season, the training for a track runner is still predominantly aerobic work. Tuesday anaerobic work is always set to current realistic goal-race pace, and never faster. i.e: if a 1500m on Sat, then Tuesday will have reps set to goal 1500m pace, after a warmup with several quality 60m strideouts, then 2000m steady lapping @ A.T. pace to warm up the anaerobic glycolytic system, then specific pace workout with full aerobic recoveries.

If an 800m race on Sat, then Tues will have the same warmup as per 1500m, but will be at 800m pace: the recoveries at 800m pace may be a lot more than for 1500m pace.

(Notice that Tuesday's 'Fast Reps' workout is tuned exactly to Saturday's 1500m goal race pace.)

Day	Overview	Details	Notes
Mon	Very easy recovery	30-40 mins easy on parkland	
Tue	Tougher effort day tuned @ current 1500m performance level or slightly faster.	5x 300m @ 48s; one every 3:00, concentrating on proper form, after suitable easy warmup with legspeed drills over 60 metres or less/ full recovery. Last one try for 45s. If more recovery needed with repetitions; may be running above one's current level. Don't run these if can't hold form. Stop session and just jog.	* As the major races approach, the emphasis of these efforts may change to more specific race-pace repetitions at exactly goal pace
Wed	Longer steady run	May range up to 70 min for seniors.	
Thu	Another effort day but not as demanding as Tue. This day is more or less kept as a constant fun speedplay day year-round.	Warmup with plenty of short fast relaxed sprints then enjoyable 'speed-play' fartleks and recoveries on undulating parkland. May be useful to have 2000m of 'steady laps' @ 75s here.(6:15).	* Alactic leg-speed day * Light fartleks and speed play according to feel, or steady lapping to practice concentration.
Frid	Very easy recovery	Usu. Over 30 mins easy on parkland	
Sat	1500m RACE or strong effort day ie: 6 x 400m @ 64s/ 1 lap recovery walk/jog. Last 400m try to pick pace up in last straight. We are "training to race, not racing to train".**Always leave something in the tank.**	Race: hold 64s to 1200m in 3:12, then position oneself for good last 150m. Training: Look for consistency of laps at expected goal race pace, with enough recovery to do repetitions with very good technique. Same w/up as Tuesday.	* Often will re-visit cross-country intervals or hill sessions when not racing. All work expected to be carried out with good rhythm and form.
Sun	Always long and very easy over hilly circuits	Juniors usually up to 90 mins if several years on programme. Older athletes often go longer, easily.	* Now the runs become quite a bit easier in intensity to offset the intensity of the harder days.

Training Week for 1:56.0 Result (VDot 69.5) (only if at that V Dot Level already!)

This workout will be nearly 10% faster than the 1500m pace workout, so much more recovery between fast repetitions should be taken. Peter Snell said he would often lie on his back with his feet up on a steeplechase barrier. The idea is to execute these repetitions with near-perfect form, so that the mind associates beautiful free-flowing sustained speed with just another day at the office. **Notice again, how Tuesday's session is exactly tuned to Saturday's goal race pace.** This is something that the Hitsystem interpretation of Lydiard is starting to understand more and more as the years go by.

Day	Overview	Details	Notes
Mon	Very easy recovery	Usu. Over 30 mins easy on parkland	
Tue	Tougher effort day tuned @ specific 800m race –pace for Saturday.	2x 400m @ 58s; full recoveries, concentrating on proper form. 5min jog then 4x200m @28-29s/ 200jog. Any variation of distances up to 600m with total work volume @800m pace usu 1200m-1600m at most.	* As the major races approach, the emphasis of these efforts may change to more specific race-pace repetitions at exactly goal pace
Wed	Longer steady easy run	May range up to 70 min on grass for seniors in summer heat.	
Thu	Another effort day but not as demanding as Tue. This day is more or less kept as a constant fun speed-play day year-round.	Warm-up with plenty of short fast relaxed sprints then enjoyable 'speed-play' fartleks and recoveries on undulating parkland	* Alactic leg-speed day * Light fartleks and speed play according to feel.
Fri	Very easy recovery	Usu. Over 30 min easy on parkland	
Sat	Morning jog; about 5 km Strong effort day or race. Very easy recovery If a race, go for a morning easy jog.	800m RACE OR *Long uphill intervals of 300m@ 5000m pace initially, lots of easy recovery as required for individual, or race-pace time trial over 600m (under 1.27) , 5 min rec jog, then 1 x 300m @ 42, good technique. Many variations possible on specific-pace work	* Often will re-visit cross-country intervals or hill sessions when not racing, as in a break from racing over Christmas-New Year. All work expected to be carried out with good rhythm and form.
Sun	Long easy recovery jog; up to 90 minutes over parkland or trails.		

Relationship of 1500m and 800m Paces to VO2 Max

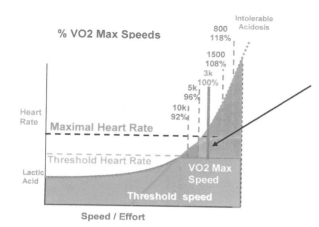

% VO2 Max Speeds

- Intolerable Acidosis
- 800 118%
- 1500 108%
- 3k 100%
- 5k 96%
- 10k 92%

Heart Rate

Maximal Heart Rate

Threshold Heart Rate

Lactic Acid

VO2 Max Speed

Threshold speed

Speed / Effort

Glycolytic (Lactate Tolerance) Exercise starts to occur here, above VO2 max speed, where lactate increases exponentially. It is best trained at 400m-600m race pace, or the fastest pace that can be maintained between 45 and 90 seconds, with complete recovery. The heart rate will often reach maximal during recovery, as it reacts to the muscular demands for oxygen. It usually won't reach maximum in a short work bout unless prior repetitions have been done.

DISTANCES: CROSS-COUNTRY

:y training varies very little from aerobic base training distances raced are heavily influenced by aerobic aining. However to master cross-country an approach n track preparation (mostly aerobic, with effort days rarely needing to be faster than 5000m paced intervals on challenging , undulating measured loops (95% VO2 max) . For many weeks it is quite safe to use a schedule like below, with the introduction of tougher cross-country intervals as well as sustained cross-country time-trials over challenging distances like 5000m, to sharpen for races that are typically 8km or over. This is only the evening programme here; your athlete will be doing early morning jogging each day too, if he or she wants to do well!

Day	Overview	Details	Notes
Mon	Very easy recovery	Usu. Over 30 mins easy on parkland	
Tue	Tougher effort day	Cross-country intervals @ high aerobic efforts/ short recoveries at cross-country race paces	Early season: Anaerobic Threshold pace intervals on cross country measured circuits: Late season: VO2 max intensities on same circuits with short recoveries.
Wed	Longer steady run	May range up to 90 min for seniors.	
Thu	Another effort day but not as demanding as Tue	Warmup with plenty of short fast relaxed sprints then strong fartleks and recoveries	* Alactic leg-speed day * CC Fartleks done with slowest runners on the inside around a circuit
Frid	Very easy recovery	Usu. Over 30 mins easy on parkland	
Sat	Strong cc effort day or race	Long high-aerobic TT or long intervals/short recovery on hilly cross-country circuits	* Often rolling 5000m efforts on a set course expected to be carried out with good rhythm and at sub-threshold levels.
Sun	Always long and very easy over hilly circuits	Juniors usually over 1 hour when able: Seniors up to 2 hours if several years on programme.	

The use of steady time-trialling over cross-country circuits will toughen the athlete's legs up! The 'core work' it imparts is ideal.

5000m & 10000m Training

Whether an athlete specializes over 800m or marathon, the base endurance period will be virtually identical on the Lydiard system. The purpose of the aerobic base for the middle distance runner is to INCREASE HIS CAPACITY TO DO MORE ANAEROBIC VOLUME, LATER, WITH FASTER RECOVERY.

The purpose of base conditioning for a marathoner is to INCREASE HIS CAPACITY TO DO MORE AEROBIC VOLUME AT HIGHER SPEEDS, WITH FASTER RECOVERY, and INCREASE UTILIZATION OF FATTY ACIDS, while CONSERVING GLYCOGEN STORES.

I have been asked often about the difference in final preparations for 5000m and 10000m to middle distance events. The 10000m, despite being twice the distance of the 5000m, is run at a speed only 4.3% slower.

Both of these events are predominantly aerobic, and have very similar energy system demands to each other, which is why there have been several Olympians over the years who have managed the "double" at one Olympics.

For these far more aerobic events, it is important that you stress the VO2 work about once a week, and balance it out with some good leg-speed work and some sub-threshold running, and the other sessions would be all easier aerobic runs, of varying lengths.

Sub-threshold runs are extremely useful for building up aerobic capacity without tearing your glycogen stores down too much. You could include a sub-threshold ('3/4 effort' run somewhere each week in your training).

As you get naturally fitter, faster, and stronger, to really maximise your times it would be useful to regularly race 800m and 1500m distances on the track as well, but you could do this very well with just VO2 Max intervals on Tuesdays, leg-speed runs on Thursdays, and 800/1500 races on Saturdays.

These hints are useful for you as you attempt 5000 and 10000m distances. Hopefully you'll know all your heart rate training zones so you can control your efforts on your harder aerobic effort days.

> 1) Long EASY runs are maintained in-season, throughout early races, until about 2 weeks before THE major competition/peak race
>
> 2) These long runs may be far more relaxed and quite a bit slower than during your base phase (ie: they can be 1 min/km slower and you will still get the aerobic/slow twitch Type I fiber stimulus you need).
>
> This is important because your more intense sessions during the week will tend to deplete your valuable glycogen stores, which we need for fast racing, and we want the aerobic running as easy, active recovery. Go for easy running time rather than distance.
>
> 3) One weekly session of VO2 max type intervals, and one steady sub-threshold run (ie: 45min-60min S.T. inserted into an 80 minute run, when not racing).
>
> 4) Do an easy morning jog (6-8k) on your interval days (this will 'warm you up' for an evening interval session, and keep an aerobic stimulus present).
>
> 5) You need very little glycolytic work (ie: 300m-400m repetitions @ 800m/1500m pace) for 5000/10000m- it can be too anaerobic to yield a benefit for essentially aerobic-dominant events. In fact if you overdo 1500m/800m-type workouts, you could find your aerobic enzyme levels drop to compensate a bit. However, something like 8 x 400m @ 5000m race-pace might be fine, with 200m jog recovery.

6) I'd only do ONE 1500-type glycolytic workout in a leadup to a 5000,about 7-10 days out from the race, with plenty of aerobic running before and after, and only once you have successfully completed several weeks of the VO2 work, AND seem to be improving well on it.

If you dig yourself into a little hole and feel more tired than you feel you should in the next days, just jog for an hour or so each day until fully recovered. It's better to be fresh and recovered and miss a planned harder session than to race tired or to 'over-reach' in training.

The 10000m is raced at a pace halfway between your VO2 Max and your Anaerobic threshold. The 5000m is run at 95% of your VO2 max. So for most of your leadup, you could get away with a strong set of intervals @ 5000m pace, with equal or shorter recovery. As you get to the last two weeks, you could make the intervals a bit faster, at 3000m pace (100% VO2 Max pace). You might do one less interval to cope with the increased intensity and recover well. To make this training fun, you could do it around a parkland loop, or on trails.

It doesn't have to be on the track. IT IS ESSENTIAL THAT YOU TRAIN AT YOUR OWN LEVEL IN ANY INTERVAL WORKOUT; a little bit too fast, and you might harm your recovery. You get stronger in your good recovery time.

WHAT NOT TO DO!

One of the guys in our training squad couldn't get it through his thick skull that his incredible ability to churn out very hard and fast 400s or 1000s on the training track was the same reason why he couldn't or wouldn't improve. His racing results were up and down like a "yo-yo"! This guy was doing anaerobic work two or three times a week that would deliver a sub 3:35 1500 to anyone else who had put in the appropriate steady aerobic volume, but he was so near his absolute limits in training that his racing was awful. This of course affected his psychology. Why did he do it? He said he "needed to run fast in training so that I feel I can race these guys!" Recently he had to have a pacemaker inserted to cope with the possible damage done to his heart.

As a young athlete you DON'T have the luxury of making big training mistakes. Time flies before you know it, and the promising 'wunderkind' can become very ordinary after several seasons of poor results and injury niggles.

BIG HINTS

It is EXTREMELY IMPORTANT that you match up your VO2 work closely to your realistic 5000m time. The safest way to get in a decent volume of work that will push up VO2 is to do your 2-3 minute intervals at YOUR 5000m pace. By now you will realize that your 5000m pace is 95% of your VO2 max pace (3000m pace), so just believe me and we'll move on!

HOW TO PUT IT TOGETHER:

Here's a sample early-season week for someone wishing to sneak under 14:00 for 5000m: remember, these workouts are useful ONLY IF YOU HAVE DEVELOPED THE AEROBIC CAPACITY and have performed at a convincing level that indicates you can "take the next step". So for the athlete ready to break 14:00, a realistic session that he should be able to complete convincingly would be 5 x 1000m/ near equal time recovery at 13:45 pace.

Make Monday-Wednesday-Friday your easier running days year-round. Wednesday can always comprise longer "bread and butter" aerobic running in the recovery zones, and Monday can be shorter to recover from Saturday and Sunday. Friday can be an "active jogging rest" day prior to a solid Saturday & Sunday.

Mon: 1 hour easy jog

Tue: **am:** 8k easy

        pm: w/up 3k easy. 10 x 'rolling start' 60m leg-speed runs, with 1-2 laps easy jog recovery. 2000m steady at anaerobic threshold to warm up anaerobic glycolytic systems, then jog 5 mins easy before: INTERVALS: 5 x 1000m @ 5k race pace (appx), 2:45 rec (ie: 1 every six minutes- easy to set watch).

Wed: 70-90 minutes very easy running on parkland or river trails.

Thurs: **am:** 8k easy

        pm: w/up 3k easy. 10 x 'rolling start' 60m leg-speed runs, with 1-2 laps easy jog recovery. Then 30 minutes light, fun fartlek on parkland, in racing shoes or track shoes. Work efforts and recoveries to suit; make sure that the surges aren't too long or hard- should be relaxed and fun. Then 15 minutes warm-down, easy.

Fri: pm: 1 hour easy jog.

Sat: am: 8k easy jog

        pm: RACE, or 80 minutes incl 45-60 mins @ sub-threshold pace (for this person: about 3:15 per km). The 80 mins would include the warm-up, progressively easing into sub-threshold, and the cooling-down.

Sun: Long very easy run 2hrs +.

Later on, you'd keep the easier days much the same, but would 'tweak' a couple of other energy systems in just to keep them all trained. So you might do your Saturday session as above, but raise the tempo to nearer your threshold, for a shorter duration. In the last weeks you may drop the long run by half an hour to freshen for your biggest races, but if run easily and appropriately the long runs should just add to the race day strength, not detract.

You might also do time-trials just to iron out psychological flat spots, on a track, for 5,000m or 10'0000m. These trials should be constant laps, and may be over minute slower than your best (5'000m) and 3 minutes slower for 10k. The key for time trials is rhythm, constancy, no real variation in lap times, and to train your concentration.

Peaking For 10,000m:

Whereas a middle distance runner or speed endurance athlete of any description will need a number of preliminary competitions over or under race distance to reach an absolute seasonal peak, this isn't necessarily so for a distance runner, for one very good reason. Short, very fast glycolytic anaerobic efforts can be recovered from very quickly by someone who has done the aerobic preparatory work, whereas long races run at a top level can drain the physiological and psychological reserves of the athlete quite a bit.

So it's a matter of keeping decent low-level aerobic volume going purely for the restorative effects, while one does the VO2 max work necessary to peak for the longer distances. The athlete could also enter races which will be shorter and faster than the race distance, as well as doing some steady work at paces slightly slower than intended race pace.

A 10,000m runner will benefit from a hard 5,000m a few weeks away from competition, with plenty of recovery, as well as a 3,000m race which will represent a specific VO2 max workout. There can be several easy running days in between specific pace workouts. Naturally, light leg-speed drills continue every week, as they should all-year round.

To balance the 3,000m training out, a 10,000m athlete will need to fit in a training effort at his or her anaerobic threshold pace, for perhaps 2 x 20 minutes with 10 minutes jogging between efforts; anaerobic threshold tempos represent full-on road race intensities, and should be regarded with caution as they can still deplete glycogen stores. The nervous system will still assimilate the workout information, even if it is just a little injection of the correct work.

Lydiard would get the athlete to do 25 laps of the track, or 10,000m, a couple of times in training, but at an intensity more approaching marathon pace., with every lap as even as possible. This was to embed the psychology of steady lapping, more than specific physiological requirements. The thinking was that if you'd trained at faster than race speeds, and at slower than race speeds to balance things out, you still wouldn't necessarily race well if you hadn't undergone the process of churning out lap after lap in practice. These are the sort of 'one percenters' that separate Lydiard's method from the rest.

10,000m pace is halfway between anaerobic threshold intensity and VO2 max intensity, so apart from steady lapping with short recoveries at exactly that pace, there is a place for 10,000m time trials at the slower pace, as well as a race or specific work at 3,000m pace. Since the 10,000m is very influenced by the aerobic processes, it would be counter-productive to do much work at faster than VO2 max pace (or 3,000m pace for most good athletes). Physiologically, 10000m intensity is represented as vΔ50, or halfway between the velocity at VO2 max pace and the velocity at anaerobic threshold pace.

If you've done the sort of work as described here in the lead-in weeks, there'd be little need for much work on the glycolytic anaerobic system specifically; some work has to be done at 800m pace and 1500m pace, naturally, to account for a fast sustained finish, but not much; maybe just one or two sessions at most. I'd prefer to practice these sustained drives to the finish in the VO2 max sessions run over 800m to 1200m distances. The pure speed element is refined year-round with the ongoing legspeed work once a week. The hill-work coming into the VO2 max work would wake up the fast twitch fibers, and a creative programme could phase in elements of the hill exercises right up to race week.

If you concentrate on the incorrect type of anaerobic work for sharpening, you'll have the glycolytic buffering capacity of an 800m Olympian, but be two laps behind at the bell before your glory lap starts.

Holding a Sustained Peak

Some athletes need to be ready for a long competitive season, and the 'Flying Kiwis' John Walker, Dick Quax, and Rod Dixon, were masters of the sustained peak.

Not many athletes have the temperament to be able to sustain a peak, but the trick is putting 'money in the bank' with a massive, long aerobic base.

The Kiwis would 'train through' the domestic southern summer, making sure they accumulated a large mileage base before picking things up a little bit with intense work for a good showing at a National Champs. Then the real aerobic work would start; perhaps 8 to 12 weeks of big aerobic volume, tempered with leg-speed work and light fartlek, or in Walker's case, many 22 mile runs with a top marathoner, where no-one would be jogging. Then there'd be a light sharpening period to absorb the work before hitting Europe.

Someone like Walker could be running at or within a second of his best in May, and still be running at that level in September, perhaps racing most weeks, or several times a week. He and Dixon used to just do ambling, easy runs through pine forests or parkland in Europe in between races, and largely take it easy, putting restorative aerobic money back in the bank all the time with very low-stress volume on forest trails. Now and again they'd do a series of sharpeners or run-throughs on a track, but generally the racing was the intense work (there is nothing more specific!).

Final Preparation Weeks for the Marathon

The Lydiard base (or build-up) is perfect for most of a marathon preparation, except that during the last 4 weeks, on a strong running day, we'd replace the sub-threshold runs with threshold (for a couple of weeks) and then if that's been successful, we'd just polish up VO2 with a couple of VO2 max sessions too. You'd gradually taper your long run miles over the last two weeks- NOT suddenly. On your effort days, you'd NEVER NEED to do any higher intensity than the first part of VO2 max training (5k pace) above. Because of the low intensity requirements, you'd hop off the training pyramid before the 800m/1500m pace zones. The faster 5k pace work brings an element of efficiency and speed reserve to your marathon without blowing the barn doors off.

In slightly more detail

The regular Lydiard buildup as outlined in the book is fine for most of a marathon preparation. In the last 4 weeks, on your selected weekly stronger running day, we'd smoothly transition up a cog and replace the strong, fun sub-threshold 1 hour (marathon-pace/75% MHR) runs with threshold runs (15k race pace/85% MHR) for a couple of consecutive weeks.

The rest of the week would be much the same as a regular base week. DON'T do the threshold runs for an hour- that's too long for most people: to get the effect you're after without knocking yourself around too much, try something like 20 mins w/up: 20 mins A.T. tempo: 20 mins cool-down. If you're particularly strong and coping with much higher easy mileage for the bulk of your training, you could add another burst of tempo to the session. The only rule here is to think of efforts above threshold as a little inoculation of what you need. If these efforts have been successful, we'd then just polish up VO2 max to get you nicely efficient. For instance, a couple of VO2 max sessions at a maximum intensity of 95% VO2 max (5k race pace) ie: for a 15 minute 5k runner, 5 x 1000m @ 3:00/3:00 jog recovery (1 every 6 mins), OR 6 x 800m @ 2:24/2:36 recovery (1 every 5 mins). No need for anything more intense than that. KEEP THINGS SIMPLE!

NEVER do more than two tough workouts in a week leading into a distance race, unless you really like gambling! Assuming you have had a long recent aerobic buildup of at least 12-weeks, or preferably longer, the last two weeks you'd taper GRADUALLY, by firstly cutting your longer runs of the week to 80% of that achieved by week 10, and the next week back to 60%. ie: your 20-mile (32k) run would become 16 miles, then the next week 12 miles (19k), before your race. If you suddenly taper by dropping long runs, you COULD experience undue fatigue- it happens commonly. So keep an EASY aerobic undercurrent going right till race day.

You should be able to train every day at a level that you know is repeatable, ad nauseam. You'd be better off by far to drop the short fast harder efforts, and replace them with constant steady long efforts of around 75% of your heart rate reserve, but well below your anaerobic threshold (usually around 85% HRR), which is right about 15k road race pace for a good distance athlete.

'Tempo runs' or 'threshold runs' have been lionized in recent years, but I totally disagree with the regular use of this type of training in an aerobic buildup. Running at threshold for any period is a bit like like hopping into a road race, and will ensure twin outcomes: glycogen depletion, and residual muscular fatigue, each time it is done. You want to BUILD UP your aerobic system and fatty acid utilization to stave off glycogen depletion as long as possible in a marathon. So keep any of that sort of intensity down to a relatively short duration that won't wipe you out .

DON'T do the threshold runs for an hour- that's too long for most people: to get the effect you're after without knocking yourself around too much, try something like 20 mins w/up: 20 mins A.T. tempo: 20 mins cool-down. If you're particularly strong and coping with much higher easy mileage for the bulk of your training, you could add another burst of tempo to the session. The only rule here is to think of efforts above threshold as a little inoculation of what you need. Sure, you're measurably increasing your aerobic ceiling so that what was previously 'anaerobic' now becomes 'aerobic', but you're leaving the true aerobic zones behind in doing it.

These runs are much the same as your marathon race pace. Good 'Marathon Conditioning' is as much about regular hour long runs at marathon pace as it is about very long runs. People often think that Lydiard conditioning is only about long slow runs. It isn't. It's about an intelligent steady increment of aerobic pace over many weeks in the hour runs, and naturally progressing from long slow Sunday runs to long faster Sunday runs- ALL IN COMFORT, then taking the pressure off the long run pace the last few weeks. Anaerobic Threshold sessions are only a good thing to do once a huge aerobic base has been built, in specific sessions, which are preceded and followed by AMPLE low-intensity recovery running.

These sessions should be safely spaced maybe a week or so apart, to allow for ample recovery, and fat, carbohydrate and protein replacement should commence immediately the session is completed. The idea is to steadily transition into the higher intensities safely without unhappy surprises, and gradually push your anaerobic threshold up 'from below' with Lydiard's time-proven constant 1 hour "3/4 effort" runs, (roughly 75% of maximum heart rate by the Karvonen method).

This is all well-covered in the HIT book on Page 54. These runs may be done once or twice a week in your build-up. This sub-threshold running is "magic" according to Kiwi marathon great and Lydiard pupil Barry Magee, and can be considered a "cornerstone" of a good aerobic build-up. Kiwi greats John Walker, Dick Quax and Rod Dixon used these runs as cornerstones for their extensive aerobic preparations for very long European track seasons.

If you're training too hard and feel a bit ordinary, it's possibly because your system is running in a mildly acidic environment (BAD!). For the regular runner who wants to check this, urine dipsticks available from the chemist are probably useful to ascertain if your operating system is running in an alkali or acid environment.

I find diluted red grape juice is a very good alkali (diluted to be slightly weaker than isotonic with regard to sugars- usually 3:1 is about right), as well as (very surprisingly to me!) tomato juice or V8 vegetable juice. The latter is a terrific post-training recovery drink. Red grape juice is a rich source of potassium and the powerful antioxidant resveratol is sourced from red grape seeds, which are usually very cheap from the vineyard door. You simply crush a few tablespoons and sprinkle them in with your breakfast if you have Muesli or mixed cereals..

Ideally you'd have 16 weeks from a good injury-free fitness base to your marathon.

HOW TO SAFELY REACH YOUR TARGET VOLUME

Often athletes who claim that they "can't do mileage" are really saying that they can't slow their training pace enough to easily cope with mileage. Once in the regular habit of running long slow distances, as the weeks go by, the running naturally gets faster and faster and faster, all *still* at aerobic speeds, with the perceived effort being largely unchanged, but with the stopwatch telling the truth.

You'll have to gradually increase your volume runs by no more than 10% running time per week, taking it really easy, till your long ones are at least 2hr 30-40, and you can do TWO mid-week ones about 1hr 30. One way of doing this that's very good is to jog or plod for 30-60 minutes as slow as possible before running your normal medium or long run circuit. What'll happen is you'll finish with quite a long run, but the sensation that you've only really run your regular course at an easy effort. Distance doesn't kill, but speed does. The first slow part has to be around 60% MHR (Karvonen) to achieve the low-end aerobic effect desired. This will just perfuse your running muscles with lovely oxygen-rich blood in a mildly alkali environment- a perfect warm-up for higher aerobic levels without depleting glycogen stores.

In your build-up you want to start running controlled 1 hour runs at sub-threshold HR on a set course, trying to chip a couple of seconds off each time. You'll find the first few weeks of volume training are quite tiring, however once those mitochondria kick in you'll be off and away. Any additional easy aerobic activity (jogging, cycling, trail-walking, swimming) will help your overall efficiency.

After taking a few weeks to steadily reach your goal levels, your typical training week could look more like this: about 10 hours of aerobic training in your key sessions. Over a few years, you'd increase your pace and volume quite naturally.

Lydiard training for the marathon therefore would be essentially the common base training period for (ideally) over 12 weeks as above, before introducing only a touch of anaerobic threshold (maybe one specific session a week: ie: warm-up 5k, AT 6k, cool-down 5k) for two consecutive weeks, then transitioning to 2 or 3 tightly controlled, evenly paced VO2 Max sessions (ie: 5 x 1000m @ 5000m pace/ equal or shorter recovery) a good week or so apart in the last few weeks. These sessions, combined with a weekly light fartlek session that includes several short relaxed sprints with ample recovery, done throughout the base period and continued through to the eve of the goal race, would train the essential energy systems enough to get the ideal outcome.

DAY	MAIN SESSION
Mon	1hr run, EASY
Tue	1hr 30m STEADY
Wed	Light fartlek 1 hour incl 6-10 short sprints
Thu	1 hr 30m STEADY
Fri	1 hour EASY
Sat	1 hour ¾ effort marathon pace within 90 minutes run.
Sun	2 hr 30m

Do very easy medium length aerobic runs on the day before and after tougher sessions.

No hard or extended long runs in the last couple of weeks generally, and no more than two VO2 sessions in a week. Any more in a week and you're dicing with marathon death. Then a controlled taper for the last 2 weeks.

TAPERING

Your taper should be gradual, and not sudden. It's an odd thing, but many people who suddenly ease up on volume aerobic training complain of feeling sleepy and fatigued on marathon day. So whatever volume you've reached in daily runs on set days by 2 weeks to go, you want to reduce to 80% by 1 week to go, and then to 60% in marathon week leading up to race day. With aerobic training, it's essential that a certain volume or aerobic undercurrent is kept up to maintain the necessary oxidative enzyme levels and mitochondria.

ie: if your Sunday long run is 20 miles, this becomes 16 miles the next week, then the next week 12 miles. Pretty obviously, all other run lengths and times would be cut down by the same amount! (Not your recovery days!)

We don't do any glycolytic /lactate tolerance training anywhere near a marathon or during base training. Those sessions are very intense, flooding the running muscles with highly acidic metabolites that soon force the exercise to cease due to the localized neuromuscular junctions going on strike. While absolutely necessary for a middle distance athlete's final preparation, the acidosis created has the distinct possibility of harming aerobic enzyme levels, glycogen and fatty acid utilization, and mitochondrial function at the expense of your marathon potential. VO2 max intervals are far longer and far less intense, (i.e.: 1000m intervals @ 5000m pace/ equal time recovery or shorter) and are much safer and more useful coming into your absolute final phase.

For a 15 min 5,000m runner this could be something like 5 x 1,000m on the road @ 3:00/3:00 active jog recovery, preferably on a non-cambered asphalt road surface. Really, your estimated 5,000m race pace (95% of absolute VO2 max pace) is the safest to develop VO2max without overdoing things. Anaerobic training is like playing with matches in a petrol station for a marathoner. These controlled VO2 interval sessions will top up the final anaerobic contribution to VO2 Max, and thereby increase efficiency at any of the aerobic, sub threshold, or threshold speeds, but they've got to be sparingly introduced AFTER those lower systems have been trained.

WHAT'S GOING ON IN THERE?

The body will adapt to anything you consistently ask it to do. With prolonged high-aerobic efforts, the resting heart rate can drop markedly with the left ventricle becoming larger, and its muscular walls becoming thicker and more powerful. (This is effectively like training up a much more powerful pump).

Every high-pressure heart beat delivers far more blood, far further, into an ever-increasing network of low-pressure web-like capillaries. Because there are now so many very fine blood vessels developing into muscle beds that have been exposed to constant perfusion, the flow rate and pressure of the oxygen-rich blood is lowered exponentially, thereby allowing the red blood cells exponentially more time to deliver their payload to an ever-increasing surface area of working muscle cells.

More oxygen and fuel can be delivered to far more muscle cells, and the resultant metabolites can be flushed away back to the liver more quickly. Eventually very long runs become like a pleasant "walk in the park" where you can play tourist as you cover favourite courses. One can almost dissociate from one's body on long runs as it becomes a long, smooth ride. This is the type of fitness you want to take into the final weeks of a marathon preparation, at your own level.

By contrast, untrained muscle cells that don't have any direct capillarization have to obtain their nutrients second-hand, or delve into anaerobic metabolism because they haven't received the necessary oxygen. An untrained muscle will generally have the usual major arteries, merging with finer arteriole beds, then merging further with a relatively small bed of even finer capillaries. Each capillary may have to be accessed and shared by several muscle cells initially, but biopsies of muscles that have been extensively trained aerobically show that the surface area of muscle cells experiencing direct capillarization can increase vastly.

An example from nature of what I am describing is the leg muscle of one of the most aerobically fit creatures on the planet-the kangaroo. This meat is almost "spongy" on first inspection, but if you look very closely you will see that it is traversed by many very fine capillaries; many more than in meats from relatively sedentary farm-raised livestock like beef cattle.

Initially in building your marathon base, you want to run long enough, about once a week, till you achieve the "tired heavy legs" stage (this represents glycogen depletion) and then run a few more miles like that, forcing your body to respond over time by utilising a higher ratio of fatty acids. Initially this "tired, heavy legs" response may kick in quite early if you're not used to decent long runs regularly. However, as you respond, it will be entirely possible to run for over 2hrs 30 at a good clip, without undue fatigue over the last few miles.

The thing NOT to do in training, especially on long runs over 2 hours, is to carbo-load with something like a power-bar or gu-gel. Many distance runners these days do that, and think it's great because they finish their training runs with that extra shot of 'juice' in the system, then wonder why they crash badly in the marathon. HOWEVER, at marathon race pace, it's all about conserving our limited glycogen stores and becoming very effective at utilizing our ample fatty acid stores.

If you want to go as far and as long as possible without hitting the wall, you must have THREE things going for you:

1. A trained ability to utilize a blend of ('unlimited') fatty acids and ('limited') carbohydrates for long periods at high aerobic levels, thereby conserving glycogen (high energy) stores for the business end of your race.

2. Sufficient hydration of the muscles to allow access to the stored glycogen. Glycogen is really an endless starchy chain of glucose molecules. It needs about twice its volume in accessible H_2O to be metabolized. So a marathoner who is ready to race will often be slightly heavier than normal.

3. The patience to start slightly slower than your intended race pace, so as to spare glycogen and come home full of running. The marathon doesn't 'start' till the 20 mile/32km mark, so go steadily till then.

The traditional "wall" that marathoners hit at around 20 miles represents the final unloading of glycogen stores from the type IIA fatigue-resistant (aerobic) fast twitch fibres as they are sequentially recruited while the slow twitch fibres have exhausted their work capacity.

HOWEVER, if one has trained the fatty acid system properly by many weeks of long runs to depletion, BY ALL MEANS use a carbohydrate gel in the last few kilometres of a race (but test it out in training at least once on one of your weekly long runs!)

Training Young Athletes:
The Marcellin College Experience

My fellow coach, John Meagher, has emplaced a very effective training routine that ticks all the Lydiard boxes, but allows for natural progression and enthusiasm in a school setting. Teenaged schoolboys and schoolgirls are often involved in a number of school sports, as well as extra-curricular activities, so the training settings have to realistically compromise with their "other lives". The job of the coach is to get the kids to enjoy their training and racing so much, as a team, that they go on with it as a sport. John is still at the pointy end of state cross-country running at 50-plus years of age, so he's a 'Pied Piper' figure to the youngsters he inspires and encourages.

John uses a lot of positive psychology to get his crack squad (the 'HIT SQUAD') to do the steady volume of work required. Each and every year the Marcellin cross country squad wins the Australian Schoolboys Team title for Under -16 Boys. This squad gets chosen to represent Australia each year in the 'World Schools Cross Country' event; usually held in a European country, where they vie for the world schoolboy teams title. There have been several high placings at the world level, including one individual winner of the cross-country title who then went on to run 3:49.6 for 1500m at age sixteen, off a primarily aerobic cross-country foundation.

It is a big thing in the sports culture at Marcellin College now to make it to the cross-country team, and John will only take boys who show up to two key sessions each week; the Tuesday cross-country high-aerobic intervals, and the hilly long Sunday run; both done in some of the beautiful river trails and parkland along Melbourne's Yarra River. John will often have squads of up to 30 young runners on an early-morning long Sunday run, and they're finished before many of their peers have woken up.

This training model is basically a cross-country training routine for most of the year, with brief forays into track-based work before major championships. John's cross-country teams have dominated Victorian and Australian inter-collegiate competition for over 15 years, and they have garnered numerous national track medals over 1500m and 3000m over the years.

In the United Kingdom, coach Alan Maddocks , of Beacon Hill Striders in Leicester, has emplaced a very similar Lydiard-based model since 2012, when he organised for me to speak to about 50 asssorted age-group runners, coaches, and parents. Within a year, with only slight modifications to the structure he'd already set up- namely more steady running and less race-pace work, his squad saw rapid improvements, with some of the lesser-lights making County sides over track or cross-country, and the best-performed youngster topping the UK Under-16 rankings over 3000m,1500m, and cross-country in his athletics life, as well as being the top in his age-group in triathlon. It's a matter of giving teenagers and coaches certainty and encouragement to repeat what all the great runners of the past used to do; steady running, and lots of it.

Years ago, Lorraine Moller started her athletics career as a 14 year old girl who could run 56 seconds for 400m on a grass track. She was started on her path by her father Gordon, who decided that running with him in the magnificent pine forests of Putaruru would help Lorraine overcome her chronic kidney infections. He called it "cleaning out her foo-foo valve".

Courtesy Lydiard Foundation

Gradually, the sickly pubescent became a strong adolescent who would go on to represent New Zealand at every distance from 800m to the marathon, with quite a swag of Commonwealth medals and one Olympic bronze, as well as 16 city marathon titles including Boston, Osaka (twice), and the Avon Women's London marathon title.

Lorraine was trained by Lydiard's 1500m Olympic medallist John Davies, who was employed in public relations by NZ Forestry, in nearby Tokoroa. She was encouraged to do as much aerobic running as she could enjoy in the forest with her father, and by mid-teens was up to 45 miles per week, or about 5 to 6 hours of training over 7 days.

This mileage base grew quite naturally without being forced, and by the time she was eighteen, training to be a physed teacher in Dunedin, she would often accompany the men on their long runs each weekend, and give a good account of herself.

This gave her the strength to run 5th in the Commonwealth Games 800m in 2:03, in 1974. This raw strength that she acquired gradually ensured a very long career at the top of the world tree, including her come-from-behind marathon bronze in Barcelona at the age of 37, and a fourth Olympic marathon at the age of 41. Then she had her daughter at age 45.

Naturally, Lydiard training is based on a progression from what the new runner can handle initially, to the surprising levels he or she can get to when they train at the optimal intensities for weeks and months.

I'll share here our very successful youth programme, which for success at the school level depends on a mentorship process, whereby older athletes run with new athletes on the squad, advising them on form and technique, as well as making sure that the youngsters are handling their longer runs.

Longer Runs:

The senior boys, aged about 16 to 18, often run over 100 kilometres a week, or about 7 hours of training time, with the long Sunday run getting out to 90 minutes, 'give or take'. We give them a basic schedule they can "grow into" as they move into adult life, and several have become successful senior competitors, following an 'enlarged' schedule from the one they followed as younger runners. They know the system, and how it works for them on a proven basis already. By adding a few kilometres here and there, and morning runs as well, they are running the larger volumes necessary for success on the international stage.

Marcellin has access to some incredibly good circuits that comprise gravel roads and bushland nearby. If a regular circuit takes the senior athletes 60 minutes, the younger runners, of varying abilities, will be encouraged to go out and back on the first half of the course long enough to be able to handle, in increments, running times like 15 minutes out and 15 back, 20 minutes out and 20 back, etc, until they are comfortably running 30 minutes out, and 30 minutes back; a full hour; at which stage they are then fit enough to tackle the full hill loop of the circuit , often trailing the senior athletes by several hundred metres but being encouraged by a designated mentor to come back and check on progress. So every age-grouper feels part of a bigger picture, no matter how small or lacking in apparent ability.

Here's a sample of what we give the boys more or less year-round, because the school competitive seasons are so complex and busy that we have to be able to bring the team up for a little mini-peak, and then put them back into more aerobic work for a few more weeks, several times a year.

Day	Overview	Details	Notes
Mon	Very easy recovery	Usu. Over 30 mins easy on parkland	
Tue	Tougher effort day	Cross-country intervals @ high efforts/ short recoveries	* Short and sharp workout which is the closest the squad will get to true extended anaerobic work for months.
Wed	Longer steady run	May range up to 90 min for seniors.	
Thu	Another effort day but not as demanding as Tue	Warmup with plenty of short fast relaxed sprints then strong fartleks and recoveries	* Alactic leg-speed day * CC Fartleks done the 'Roger Robinson' way with slowest on the inside around a circuit
Frid	Very easy recovery	Usu. Over 30 mins easy on parkland	
Sat	Strong cc effort day or race	Long high-aerobic TT or long intervals/short recovery on hilly cross-country circuits	* Often rolling 5000m efforts on a set course expected to be carried out with good rhythm and at sub-threshold levels.
Sun	Always long and very easy over hilly circuits	Juniors usually over 1 hour when able: Seniors up to 2 hours if several years on programme.	

It doesn't take much from a good all-round fitness base like this to step things up for a competition, before rebuilding again.

Here's a sample of the type of work that's done coming out of winter and into the summer athletics season; there's a variety of low-intensity high-aerobic or a small but pivotal amount of VO2 max interval running done, on fun cross-country loops that take in bushland and little hills.

Lydiard made a point of not giving youngsters much intense work at all, preferring to develop their aerobic systems with as much enjoyable group training as possible. The very intense work, as we know, promotes systemic acidosis, which can lead to glandular fever, or its variant 'mononucleosis', ('mono'), the disease which was almost a rite of passage until recent years in North American High School athletics.

Day	Overview	Details	Notes
Mon	Very easy recovery	Usu. Over 30 mins easy on parkland	
Tue	Tougher effort day	VO2 max track intervals @ high efforts/ short recoveries, concentrating on proper form	* As the major races approach, the emphasis of these efforts may change to more specific race-pace repetitions at exactly goal pace
Wed	Longer steady run	May range up to 90 min for seniors.	
Thu	Another effort day but not as demanding as Tue	Warmup with plenty of short fast relaxed sprints then strong fartleks and recoveries	* Alactic leg-speed day * Light fartleks and speed play according to feel.
Frid	Very easy recovery	Usu. Over 30 mins easy on parkland	
Sat	Strong cc effort day or race	Long high-aerobic TT or long intervals/short recovery on hilly cross-country circuits	* Often rolling 5000m efforts on a set course expected to be carried out with good rhythm and at sub-threshold levels.
Sun	Always long and very easy over hilly circuits	Juniors usually over 1 hour when able: Seniors up to 90 mins if several years on programme.	* Now the runs become quite a bit easier in intensity to offset the increased intensity of the harder days.

Anyone can give a talented youngster a mish-mash of confused training and get a great result on occasion, but so could the school crossing lady; only she'd be kinder on their young physiologies and probably do better. I'd go so far as to say that in my limited experience of observing, reading about and listening to 'top' national-level coaches, that very few of them know how to put a season together safely and correctly, let alone see where things fit into the big picture. Very little of what they do fits into a logical progression when viewed with Lydiard-based eyes. Unfortunately, far too many keen, talented youngsters who could become world-class competitors become disheartened and injured before leaving the sport forever.

This is happening right now in all Western countries that have shied away from steady state endurance preparations.

With the Lydiard system, and hopefully my Hitsystem way of doing things, more and more youngsters will be able to get to the levels they're capable of. Finally; here's how we'd beef things up a step for youngsters who have reached a good level of training; this sort of training is identical to the type explored earlier, but you'll see the progression a bit more here.

MARCELLIN COLLEGE LATE SUMMER 1500m TRAINING for a boy capable of 4:00 for 1500m (64s/lap).

Day	Overview	Details	Notes
Mon	Very easy recovery	Usu. Over 30 mins easy on parkland	
Tue	Tougher effort day tuned @ specific race –pace for Saturday.	W/up with 6-10x alactic stride: 2000m @ 6:15 , 6x 400m @ 64s; full recoveries, concentrating on proper form.	* As the major races approach, the emphasis of these efforts may change to more specific race-pace repetitions at exactly goal pace
Wed	Longer steady run	May range up to 90 min for seniors.	Very easy and enjoyable
Thu	Another effort day but not as demanding as Tue. This day is more or less kept as a constant fun speedplay day year-round.	Warmup with plenty of short fast relaxed sprints then enjoyable 'speed-play' fartleks and recoveries on undulating parkland	* Alactic leg-speed day * Light fartleks and speed play according to feel.
Frid	Very easy recovery	Usu. Over 30 mins easy on parkland	
Sat	RACE or strong time-trial effort day (1200m @just a fraction slower than goal pace) or 1500m race. We are "training to race, not racing to train".Always leave something in the tank.	Look for extreme consistency of laps at just slower than expected race pace; ie; a 4:00m 1500m runner should be able to easily time-trial 1200m at 3:15 in training.	* Often will re-visit cross-country intervals or hill sessions when not racing. All work expected to be carried out with good rhythm and form.
Sun	Always long and very easy over hilly circuits	Juniors usually over 1 hour when able: Seniors up to 90 mins if several years on programme.	* Now the runs become quite a bit easier in intensity to offset the intensity of the harder days.

In summary: we only need to do our anaerobic work at or just above the speed of our target race. Any faster is a waste of time and effort. What WILL get you to the race result you desire is a MOUNTAIN of steady, enjoyable aerobic training, with the final topping being a few weeks of the anaerobic work we've been describing here. An aerobically fit runner is only weeks away from a top performance, and the anaerobic sessions will be 'easy'.

Hop Off the "Intensity Escalator" at or just above the level you're training for

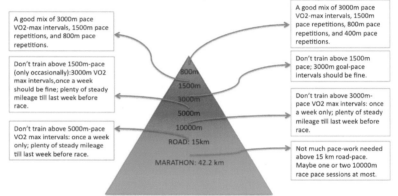

A good mix of 3000m pace VO2-max intervals, 1500m pace repetitions, and 800m pace repetitions.

Don't train above 1500m-pace (only occasionally):3000m VO2 max intervals,once a week should be fine; plenty of steady mileage till last week before race.

Don't train above 5000m-pace VO2 max intervals: once a week only; plenty of steady mileage till last week before race.

A good mix of 3000m pace VO2-max intervals, 1500m pace repetitions, 800m pace repetitions, and 400m pace repetitions.

Don't train above 1500m pace; 3000m goal-pace intervals should be fine.

Don't train above 3000m-pace VO2 max intervals: once a week only; plenty of steady mileage till last week before race.

Not much pace-work needed above 15 km road-pace. Maybe one or two 10000m race pace sessions at most.

800m
1500m
3000m
5000m
10000m
ROAD: 15km
MARATHON: 42.2 km

These principles apply for the majority of sharpening work done coming into competition on the track or road. A tiny amount of higher intensity work will be of value only for final sharpening, for an experienced athlete and coach. Remember that whenever you're training much above the anaerobic threshold, you're going into a competition between two muscle fibre types and their energy systems; too much training of one type will effectively 'de-train' the other. Any perceived inadequacies in pure SPEED and efficiency will be addressed by the fine neuro-motor coordination developed by leg-speed drills and fartlek run year-round.

Champions Are Everywhere Training Planner
Dr Keith Livingstone

How to Use the Hitsystem Training Planner

The Lydiard system originally consisted of two training cycles per year, neatly divided into two 26-week halves. It is a good idea to use the home training base during winter to build up the aerobic base, toughening the whole body to handle the hard work required for a personal best.

World class British athletes such as Steve Cram, Seb Coe, Steve Ovett and Peter Elliott all turned out regularly for their clubs in winter. John Walker ran 4th in the world cross-country championships in the year he broke the 3:50 mile barrier.

This simple planner has general preparation phases colour-coded to match the Phase preparation pages in the 'Champions Are Everywhere' book. Use it to plan a general overview of your seasons, 'Lydiard-style'.

You'll notice that only eight weeks are included for an aerobic buildup phase in this diary. This is to allow for more than enough very low-level recovery from the previous season's top-end training and performances. You may, of course, start your aerobic buildup earlier if you are able to.

The longer aerobic buildup will power you deeper into a season of racing, and Kiwi marathon great Kevin Ryan used to say that whenever he "did 12 weeks of buildup, by myself, I'd come out of it as a different creature".

PHASE COLOUR CODES & MATCHING PHASE PAGES.(refer Pg 25).

PHASE	Description
Active Recovery	Informal fitness work
Aerobic Base	Pg 22-24
Ph II: Hill Exercises	Pg 28-33
Ph III: VO2 Max	Pg 40-42
Ph IV: Glycolytic Anaerobic	Pg 43-46

All you have to do is plot your workouts according to the general outline given on page 25, working backwards from a realistic goal on a certain date, and fill in the progressive workouts on the usual workout or race days of Tuesdays and Saturdays, keeping Thursdays to the staple leg-speed drills (neuromuscular work) and light fartlek routine. This calendar can obviously be used for winter (higher mileage without the track-style peak), or for summer racing. It can also be used for other endurance sports, where you'd plan your workouts similarly with regard to workout intensities, and where event-specific resistance work would replace the hill exercises. These sheets will give you the overview; you can pen in the final details as you go through the season.

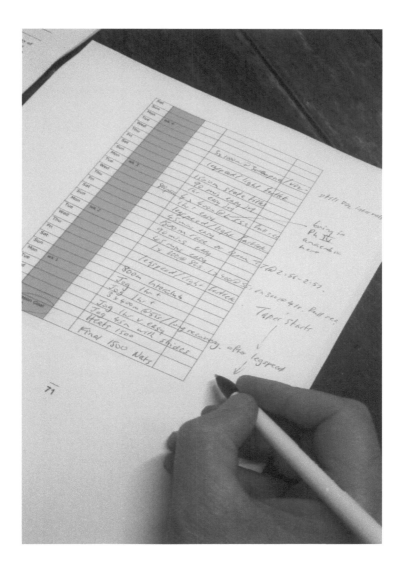

Just enter in the workout details in the appropriate phases, and fill in the 'blanks' of recovery days on Mondays, Wednesdays, Fridays, Sundays. For other endurance sports, the same principles apply: A kayaker can tow a fishing net with fishing floats or inflated balls for the resistance phase; a cyclist can choose a short steep incline and go up it in the largest gear.

		Phase	Workout	Date
Day			**General Recovery and pre-season work**	
Mon	Wk26			
Tue			moderate effort	
Wed			Long easy recovery	
Thu			light work incl neuromuscular	
Fri			light recovery	
Sat			moderate effort	
Sun			longer moderate effort	
Mon	wk25		light recovery	
Tue			moderate effort	
Wed			Long easy recovery	
Thu			light work incl neuromuscular	
Fri			light recovery	
Sat			moderate effort	
Sun			longer moderate effort	
Mon	wk24		light recovery	
Tue			moderate effort	
Wed			Long easy recovery	
Thu			light work incl neuromuscular	
Fri			light recovery	
Sat			moderate effort	
Sun			longer moderate effort	
Mon	wk23		light recovery	
Tue			moderate effort	
Wed			Long easy recovery	
Thu			light work incl neuromuscular	
Fri			light recovery	
Sat			moderate effort	
Sun			longer moderate effort	

Mon	wk22		light recovery	
Tue			moderate effort	
Wed			Long easy recovery	
Thu			light work incl neuromuscular	
Fri			light recovery	
Sat			moderate effort	
Sun			longer moderate effort	
Mon	wk 21		**Insert base-building workouts from here on**	
Tue				
Wed				
Thu				
Fri				
Sat				
Sun				
Mon	wk20			
Tue				
Wed				
Thu				
Fri				
Sat				
Sun				
Mon	wk19			
Tue				
Wed				
Thu				
Fri				
Sat				
Sun				
Mon	wk18			
Tue				
Wed				

Thu				
Fri				
Sat				
Sun				
Mon	wk17			
Tue				
Wed				
Thu				
Fri				
Sat				
Sun				
Mon	wk16			
Tue				
Wed				
Thu				
Fri				
Sat				
Sun				
Mon	wk15			
Tue				
Wed				
Thu				
Fri				
Sat				
Sun				
Mon	wk14			
Tue				
Wed				
Thu				
Fri				
Sat				

Sun				
Mon	wk13			
Tue				
Wed				
Thu				
Fri				
Sat				
Sun				
Mon	wk12			
Tue				
Wed				
Thu				
Fri				
Sat				
Sun				
Mon	wk11			
Tue				
Wed				
Thu				
Fri				
Sat				
Sun				
Mon	Wk 10			
Tue				
Wed				
Thu				
Fri				
Sat				
Sun				
Mon	wk 9			
Tue				

Wed				
Thu				
Fri				
Sat				
Sun				
Mon	wk 8			
Tue				
Wed				
Thu				
Fri				
Sat				
Sun				
Mon	wk 7			
Tue				
Wed				
Thu				
Fri				
Sat				
Sun				
Mon	wk 6	Final Phase		
Tue				
Wed				
Thu				
Fri				
Sat				
Sun				
Mon	wk 5			
Tue				
Wed				
Thu				
Fri				

Sat				
Sun				
Mon	wk 4			
Tue				
Wed				
Thu				
Fri				
Sat				
Sun				
Mon	wk 3			
Tue				
Wed				
Thu				
Fri				
Sat				
Sun				
Mon	wk 2			
Tue				
Wed				
Thu				
Fri				
Sat				
Sun				
Mon	wk 1			
Tue				
Wed				
Thu				
Fri				
Sat	Season Goal Race			

CPSIA information can be obtained
at www.ICGtesting.com
Printed in the USA
LVHW071557241122
733973LV00001B/1